Pearson
Revise

Pearson Edexcel GCSE (9–1)
Mathematics
Foundation tier
Ten-Minute Tests

T0346308

Series Consultant: Harry Smith

Authors: Ian Bettison and Su Nicholson

These Ten-Minute Tests are designed to complement your revision, providing quick tests of the core knowledge and skills you will need for your exams, allowing you to identify the areas in which you are strong and any areas where you could improve through further practice. They are not representative of a real exam paper. Remember that the official Pearson specification and associated assessment guidance materials are the only authoritative source of information and should always be referred to for definitive guidance.

For the full range of Pearson revision titles across KS2, 11+, KS3, GCSE, Functional Skills, AS/A Level and BTEC visit: www.pearsonschools.co.uk/revise

Published by Pearson Education Limited, 80 Strand, London, WC2R 0RL.

www.pearsonschoolsandfecolleges.co.uk

Copies of official specifications for all Pearson qualifications may be found on the website: qualifications.pearson.com

Text and illustrations © Pearson Education Ltd 2020
Typeset and illustrated by Newgen KnowledgeWorks Pvt. Ltd., Chennai, India
Produced by Newgen Publishing UK
Cover illustration by Miriam Sturdee

The rights of Ian Bettison and Su Nicholson to be identified as authors of this work have been asserted by them in accordance with the Copyright, Designs and Patents Act 1988.

First published 2020

24
10 9 8 7 6

British Library Cataloguing in Publication Data
A catalogue record for this book is available from the British Library

ISBN 978 1 2922 9431 5

Printed and bound in Great Britain by Bell and Bain Ltd, Glasgow

Notes from the publisher

1. While the publishers have made every attempt to ensure that advice on the qualification and its assessment is accurate, the official specification and associated assessment guidance materials are the only authoritative source of information and should always be referred to for definitive guidance.

Pearson examiners have not contributed to any sections in this resource relevant to examination papers for which they have responsibility.

2. Pearson has robust editorial processes, including answer and fact checks, to ensure the accuracy of the content in this publication, and every effort is made to ensure this publication is free of errors. We are, however, only human, and occasionally errors do occur. Pearson is not liable for any misunderstandings that arise as a result of errors in this publication, but it is our priority to ensure that the content is accurate. If you spot an error, please do contact us at resourcescorrections@pearson.com so we can make sure it is corrected.

How to use this book

This book is designed to help you test yourself on the knowledge and skills you will need for your Pearson Edexcel Foundation GCSE Mathematics exam. The book contains 46 short tests, covering the whole of your specification and you should spend 10 minutes on each test.

Easy-to-use answers with hints, marking tips and working will allow you to mark your tests quickly and accurately. This will help to boost your confidence in areas where you get a high mark. It will also help you to plan your revision effectively by focusing on the areas in which you get a lower mark and could improve with further practice. Some extra pointers are given at the end of each test to help you develop your personal revision plan.

If you have the Revise Pearson Edexcel GCSE (9–1) Mathematics Revision Guide you can follow the links at the top of each test for more help with that topic.

1 Look out for these **core skill** questions – these skills and topics come up year after year so make sure you are confident with them.

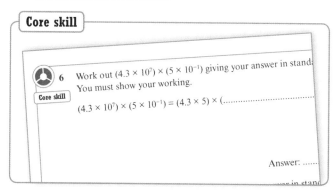

2 Look at this **scale** next to each question in a test. It will tell you how difficult the question is.

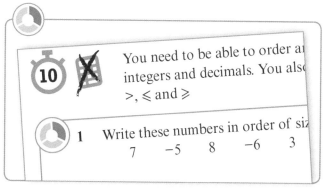

3 Use the **QR code** to jump straight to the answers, or go to the back of the book. Use the **hints** in the answers to help you understand any questions you answered incorrectly.

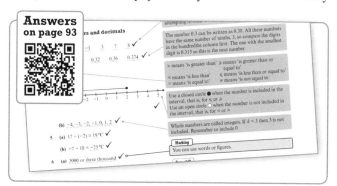

4 Record your mark for each question in the box next to the question. Then total your number of marks for the whole test at the bottom of the right-hand page.

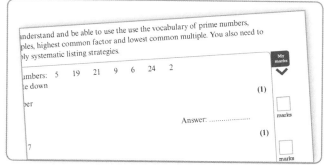

5 Use your score to help you **plan** your revision. If you need more help, look at the Revise Pearson Edexcel GCSE (9–1) Mathematics Revision Guide

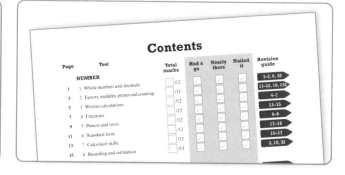

6 Use the contents page to **record** your test scores. Create your own revision plan by ticking the boxes to show your confidence level with every topic across the whole specification.

Contents

A small bit of small print

Pearson Edexcel publishes Sample Assessment Material and the Specification on its website. This is the official content and this book should be used in conjunction with it. The questions have been written to help you revise topics and practise the skills you will need in your exam.

Remember – the real exam questions may not look like this.

1 Whole numbers and decimals

10 ✗ You need to be able to order and apply the four operations to positive and negative integers and decimals. You also need to understand and be able to use the symbols =, ≠, <, >, ≤ and ≥

1 Write these numbers in order of size from smallest to largest.

7   −5   8   −6   3   −1   **(1)**

Answer: ....

My marks

☐ marks

2 Write these numbers in order of size from smallest to largest.

0.32   0.315   0.3   0.36   0.374   **(1)**

Answer: ....

☐ marks

3 Choose the correct symbol to complete this statement:

5.7 + 1.4 ☐ 7.8 − 0.9

Tick **one** box.   **(1)**

☐ **A** <   ☐ **B** ≤   ☐ **C** =   ☐ **D** ≥   ☐ **E** >

☐ marks

4 (a) The number n is such that $-3 < n \leqslant 2$

Show this on the number line.   **(1)**

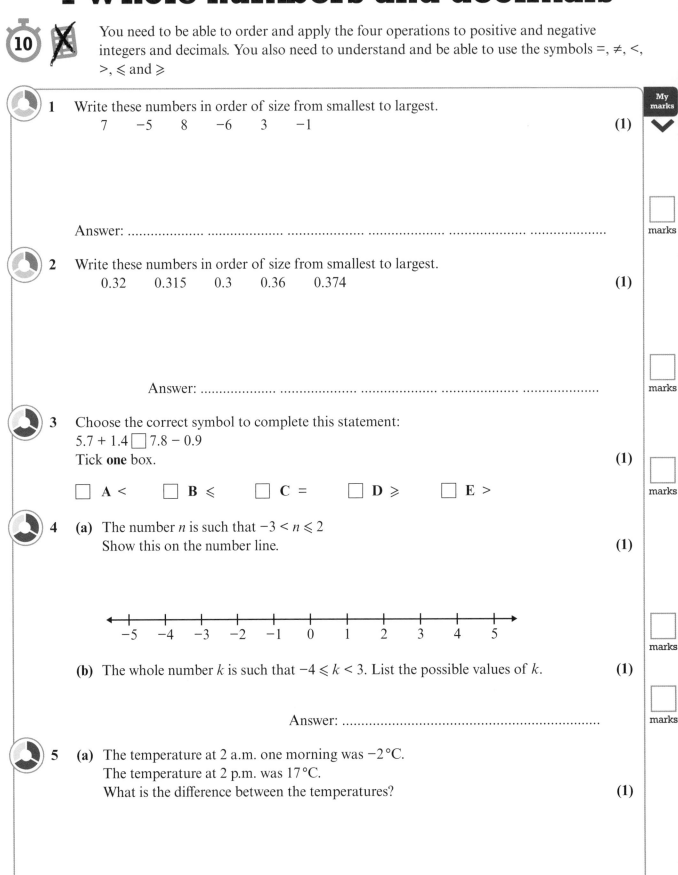

(b) The whole number k is such that $-4 \leqslant k < 3$. List the possible values of k.   **(1)**

Answer: ....

☐ marks

☐ marks

5 (a) The temperature at 2 a.m. one morning was −2 °C.

The temperature at 2 p.m. was 17 °C.

What is the difference between the temperatures?   **(1)**

Answer: ....°C

☐ marks

(b) During a climb of Mount Everest, the temperature at the base was −7 °C.
The temperature at the summit was 18 °C colder.
What was the temperature at the summit? **(1)**

Answer: .... °C

6 (a) What is the value of the 3 in 203 560? **(1)**

Answer: ....

(b) What is four million, three hundred and twenty-six thousand in figures? **(1)**

- [ ] **A** 43 260
- [ ] **B** 432 600
- [ ] **C** 4 326 000
- [ ] **D** 43 260 000

7 Work out $14 - 3 \times 5 + 2$
Tick **one** box. **(1)**

Core skill

- [ ] **A** 1
- [ ] **B** 57
- [ ] **C** 77
- [ ] **D** −3

8 Find the number that is exactly halfway between −5 and 11 **(2)**

Answer: ....

My marks

marks

marks

marks

marks

marks

Make a plan

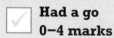 **Had a go**
0–4 marks
Recap working with place value and with negative numbers, before tackling the core skill of applying the four operations in the correct order to all numbers including decimals.

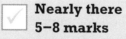 **Nearly there**
5–8 marks
Well done! Use the hints in the answers to work out where you could have picked up more marks. Make sure you know the difference between the different inequality signs and how to use them.

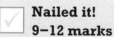 **Nailed it!**
9–12 marks
Congratulations! Being able to work with whole numbers and decimals confidently will help you answer word problems and statistics questions.

MY TOTAL MARKS

Answers on page 93

2 Factors, multiples, primes and counting

  You need to understand and be able to use the use the vocabulary of prime numbers, factors, multiples, highest common factor and lowest common multiple. You also need to be able to apply systematic listing strategies.

My marks ⌄

1 Here is a list of numbers: 5   19   21   9   6   24   2
From this list write down

(a) a prime number   **(1)**

Answer: ....

☐ marks

(b) a multiple of 7   **(1)**

Answer: ....

☐ marks

(c) a factor of 54   **(1)**

Answer: ....

☐ marks

2 Complete the factor tree to write 84 as the product of its prime factors.
Give your answer in index form.   **(2)**

84
⟨ 2 ⟩   42

Answer: ....

☐ marks

3 Use your answer to Question 2 and complete the working and Venn diagram at the top of the next page to help you work out the highest common factor (HCF) of 84 and 180   **(3)**

Core skill

As a product of its prime factors 180 = ...

My marks

Prime factors of 84

Prime factors of 180

Answer: HCF = ...

marks

4 Use your answer to Question 3 to help you work out the lowest common multiple (LCM) of 84 and 180

Core skill

(1)

Answer: LCM = ...

marks

5 A netball league contains 6 teams.

Aces   Cobras   Diamonds
Hot Shots   Magpies   Thunderbolts

Each team must play each of the other teams once.
How many matches will be played in total?
You must show your working.

(2)

Answer: ....

marks

Make a plan

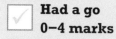 **Had a go**
0–4 marks
Revise working with factors, multiples and primes and Venn diagrams to help with the core skills of finding highest common factors and lowest common multiples.

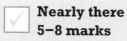 **Nearly there**
5–8 marks
Well done! Use the hints in the answers to work out where you could have picked up more marks. It might also help to recap efficient counting strategies.

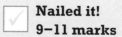 **Nailed it!**
9–11 marks
Congratulations! Keep an eye out for the use of Venn diagrams in probability questions as well.

 MY TOTAL MARKS

 **Answers on page 94**

3 Written calculations

 You need to be able to apply the four operations to integers and decimals, and to understand and be able to use place value.

1 Use a number line to work out

(a) 358 + 47 **(1)**

358

Answer: .... marks

(b) 185 − 56 **(1)**

+—————————————————————
56

Answer: .... marks

 2 436 × 24 = 10 464

Use this information to write down the value of

Core skill

(a) 4.36 × 24 **(1)**

Answer: .... marks

(b) 10 464 ÷ 2.4 **(1)**

Answer: .... marks

 3 (a) Complete the working to calculate 7.6 × 0.08 **(2)**

$$\begin{array}{r} 76 \\ \times\ 8 \\ \hline \\ \hline \end{array}$$

Answer: .... marks

(b) What is the value of the 8 in the number 0.08? **(1)**

Answer: $\dfrac{8}{\boxed{}}$

marks

4 Complete the working to calculate $44.8 \div 1.6$ **(2)**

$$\frac{44.8}{1.6} = \frac{\boxed{}}{16}$$

$$16\overline{\smash{)}\boxed{}}^{\boxed{}}$$

Answer: ....

marks

5 Work out 461×58 **(3)**

Answer: ....

marks

4 Fractions

  You need to be able to add, subtract, multiply and divide fractions and mixed numbers **without** using a calculator.

1 What fraction is equivalent to $\frac{2}{3}$? (1)
Tick **one** box.

☐ **A** $\frac{3}{4}$

☐ **B** $\frac{4}{5}$

☐ **C** $\frac{4}{6}$

☐ **D** $\frac{5}{6}$

My marks ☐ marks

2 Work out $\frac{2}{3} + \frac{1}{4}$
Tick **one** box. (1)

☐ **A** $\frac{3}{7}$

☐ **B** $\frac{3}{12}$

☐ **C** $\frac{10}{12}$

☐ **D** $\frac{11}{12}$

☐ marks

3 Work out $\frac{3}{5}$ of 120
Tick **one** box. (1)

☐ **A** 24

☐ **B** 40

☐ **C** 72

☐ **D** 200

☐ marks

4 Work out $12 \div \frac{3}{4}$ (2)

Core skill

Answer: ....

☐ marks

5 Complete the working to work out $2\frac{3}{5} + 3\frac{1}{2}$ (2)

Core skill

$2\frac{3}{5} = \frac{\square}{5}$ $3\frac{1}{2} = \frac{\square}{2}$

$2\frac{3}{5} + 3\frac{1}{2} = \frac{.................}{10}$

Answer: ....

☐ marks

6 Work out $2\frac{1}{3} \times 3\frac{3}{4}$

Give your answer as a mixed number. (2)

My marks ⌄

Answer: ....

☐ marks

7 A glass holds $\frac{1}{3}$ litre of water.

How many full glasses can be filled from a $3\frac{1}{2}$ litre jug of water? (3)

Number of full glasses ....

☐ marks

Make a plan

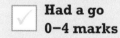 **Had a go**
0–4 marks

Revise operations on fractions. Focus on the core skills of finding a common denominator to add and subtract fractions and the methods for multiplication and division.

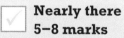 **Nearly there**
5–8 marks

Well done! Remember that if a question asks you to give your answer in its simplest form, you need to make sure you identify any common factors in the numerator and denominator – it's a core skill that you need to master.

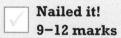 **Nailed it!**
9–12 marks

Congratulations! Keep an eye out for use of fractions in worded questions as well – you might need to pick which operation is appropriate for a particular question, or use your knowledge of percentages and ratio together with fractions.

☐ **MY TOTAL MARKS**

Answers on page 96

5 Powers and roots

 You need to be able to calculate with roots and with integer indices.

1 Work out

(a) $\sqrt{121}$ **(1)**

Answer: ....

(b) $\sqrt[3]{64}$ **(1)**

Answer: ....

2 Write down the value of

(a) 5^0 **(1)**

Answer: ....

(b) 5^{-2} **(1)**

Answer: ....

(c) $100 - (-4)^3$ **(1)**

Answer: ....

3 Write as a single power of 3

 (a) $3^5 \times 3^3$ **(1)**

Answer: ....

(b) $(3^2)^3$ (1)

Answer: .... marks

(c) $\dfrac{3^4 \times 3^2}{3}$ (1)

Answer: .... marks

4 Complete the working to find the value of $\left(\dfrac{2}{5}\right)^{-3}$ (2)

$$\left(\dfrac{2}{5}\right)^{-3} = \left(\dfrac{\square}{\square}\right)^{3}$$

Answer: .... marks

5 Work out the value of $\left(\sqrt{3}\right)^4$
You must show your working.

$\left(\sqrt{3}\right)^4 = $ .... $\times$ .... $\times$ .... $\times$ .... (2)

Answer: .... marks

Make a plan

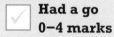 **Had a go**
0–4 marks

Recap your work on squares, cubes and roots. You should remember squares up to 15 × 15 and the corresponding square roots, and the cubes of 2, 3, 4, 5 and 10 and the corresponding cube roots.

 Nearly there
5–8 marks

Well done! Make sure you learn the laws of indices and are confident applying them – they won't be given to you in the exam.

 Nailed it!
9–12 marks

Congratulations! The laws of indices apply to algebra as well as to numbers, so practising them will help with lots of different question types.

 MY TOTAL MARKS

Answers on page 97

6 Standard form

10 You need to be able to calculate with and interpret numbers written in standard form.
Numbers in standard form can be written as $A \times 10^n$, where $1 \leqslant A < 10$ and n is an integer.

1 Write 65 000 in standard form. **(1)**

Answer: ....

marks

2 Write 5.2×10^5 as an ordinary number. **(1)**

Answer: ....

marks

3 Write 0.000 43 in standard form. **(1)**

Answer: ....

marks

4 Write the following numbers in order of size.
Start with the smallest number. **(1)**
2.6×10^3 2.6   260 2.6×10^{-5}

Answer: ....

marks

5 Work out $(6.7 \times 10^6) + (3.4 \times 10^5)$ giving your answer in standard form.
You must show your working. **(2)**

Core skill

$6.7 \times 10^6 = $ ....

$3.4 \times 10^5 = $ ....

Answer: ....

marks

6 Work out $(4.3 \times 10^7) \times (5 \times 10^{-1})$ giving your answer in standard form. You must show your working. **(2)**

Core skill

$(4.3 \times 10^7) \times (5 \times 10^{-1}) = (4.3 \times 5) \times (\dots\dots\dots\dots\dots\dots\dots\dots\dots\dots\dots\dots\dots)$

Answer: .... marks

7 Work out $(1.4 \times 10^{-5}) \div (2 \times 10^{-2})$ giving your answer in standard form. You must show your working. **(2)**

$(1.4 \times 10^{-5}) \div (2 \times 10^{-2}) = (1.4 \div 2) \times (\dots\dots\dots\dots\dots\dots\dots\dots\dots\dots\dots\dots\dots)$

Answer: .... marks

8 The distance between the Earth and the Moon is approximately 4×10^5 km. The distance between the Earth and the Sun is approximately 1.5×10^8 km.
Use this information to work out how many times further it is from the Earth to the Sun than from the Earth to the Moon. **(2)**

Answer: .... marks

Make a plan

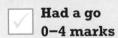 **Had a go**
0–4 marks

Revise work on writing ordinary numbers in standard form and vice versa before tackling the core skill of calculating with numbers in standard form without using a calculator.

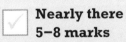 **Nearly there**
5–8 marks

Well done! Use the hints in the answers to work out where you could have picked up more marks. Read questions carefully to make sure you give your answer in the specified form.

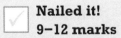 **Nailed it!**
9–12 marks

Congratulations! Make sure you are confident doing operations on standard form numbers both with and without a calculator.

 MY TOTAL MARKS

Answers
on page 97

Revision Guide pages 16, 17

7 Calculator skills

  You need to be able to calculate with roots and with integer indices. You also need to be able to use your calculator to carry out operations on numbers given in standard form.

1 Work out 6.25^2 **(1)**

Answer: .... marks

2 Find $\sqrt{15.21}$ **(1)**

Answer: .... marks

3 **(a)** Find the value of the reciprocal of 3.2
Give your answer as a decimal. **(1)**

Answer: .... marks

(b) Work out the value of $\dfrac{1}{6.4 \times 10^{-3}}$ **(1)**

Answer: .... marks

4 Find the value of $(3.6 - 0.55)^2 + \sqrt[3]{10.648}$
You must show your working. **(2)**

$(3.6 - 0.55)^2 = ...$

$\sqrt[3]{10.648} = ...$

Answer: .... marks

5 Find the value of $\dfrac{\sqrt{12.5 + 3.4}}{4.2^3}$

Write down all the figures on your calculator display.
You must show your working. **(2)**

$\sqrt{12.5 + 3.4}$ = ...

4.2^3 = ...

Answer: .... marks

6 Work out $(3.72 \times 10^{-4}) \times (2.1 \times 10^7)$
Give your answer in standard form. **(2)**

Core skill

Answer: .... marks

7 Work out the value of $\dfrac{2.625 \times 10^5}{5.25 \times 10^{-3}}$

Give your answer in standard form. **(2)**

Core skill

Answer: .... marks

My marks

Make a plan

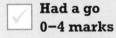 **Had a go**
0–4 marks

Practise with your calculator to make sure you know how to enter standard form numbers and fractions.

 Nearly there
5–8 marks

Well done! Remember to use the correct order of operations, and write down your working even when you use a calculator.

 Nailed it!
9–12 marks

Congratulations! If you can use your calculator confidently you will save time in geometry and statistics questions.

 MY TOTAL MARKS

 Answers on page 98

8 Rounding and estimation

You need to be able to use standard units of mass, length, time, money and other measures, as well as estimate answers and check calculations using approximation and estimation. You should also be able to use inequality notation to write simple error intervals.

1 Round 56.4917 to 2 decimal places. **(1)**

Answer: ....

2 Round these weights to 3 significant figures.

(a) 13 541 g **(1)**

Answer: ....

(b) 0.001 256 3 kg **(1)**

Answer: ....

3 Work out an estimate for $\dfrac{5.23 \times 3.47}{0.472}$

Core skill You must show your working. **(2)**

$5.23 \approx$ ....

$3.47 \approx$ ....

$0.472 \approx$ ....

Answer: ....

4 The height of a cupboard is 95 cm correct to the nearest 5 cm. What is the least possible height of the cupboard? **(1)**

Answer: .... cm

5 The capacity, C, of a jug is 160 ml correct to the nearest ml. Write down the error interval for C. **(2)**

Core skill

maximum capacity = ... ml

minimum capacity = ... ml

Answer: ....

My marks ∨

marks

marks

marks

marks

marks

marks

My marks

6 Debbie organised a coffee morning for charity.
Tickets for the coffee morning cost £9.95 each.
Debbie sold 28 tickets.

(a) Work out an estimate for the money she received from the sale of the tickets. **(1)**

Answer: £ .... marks

Debbie paid £160 in costs out of the money she received from the sale of the tickets.
She gave the rest of the money to charity.

(b) Use your answer to part (a) to work out an estimate for the amount of money she
gave to charity. **(1)**

Answer: £ .... marks

(c) Which statement correctly describes your estimate?
Tick **one** box. **(1)**

My answer to part (b) is

☐ **A** an overestimate because my answer to part (a) is an underestimate
☐ **B** an underestimate because my answer to part (a) is an underestimate
☐ **C** an overestimate because my answer to part (a) is an overestimate
☐ **D** an underestimate because my answer to part (a) is an overestimate

marks

7 Ellie uses a calculator to find the value of a number n. She wrote down the first two digits of
the answer on her calculator. She wrote down 5.3
Write down the error interval for n. **(2)**

Answer: .... marks

9 Algebraic expressions

You need to be able to simplify algebraic expressions and substitute into simple formulae.

1 Simplify $x + x$ (1)

Answer: ....

2 Find the expression that is equal to $x \times x \times x$
Tick **one** box. (1)

- [ ] **A** $3x$
- [ ] **B** x^3
- [ ] **C** $3x^3$
- [ ] **D** $\sqrt[3]{x}$

3 Find the expression that is equal to $a \times b$
Tick **one** box. (1)

- [ ] **A** $2ab$
- [ ] **B** $a + b$
- [ ] **C** ab
- [ ] **D** $\dfrac{a}{b}$

4 Simplify $4x + 2x$ (1)

Answer: ....

5 Simplify $3x + 2y - y + 4x$ (1)

Core skill

Answer: ....

6 Simplify $x^4 \times x^7$ (1)

Answer: ....

7 Simplify $(x^2)^5$ (1)

Answer: ....

8 Work out the value of $4x$ when $x = 3$ (1)

Core skill

Answer: ....

My marks

marks

marks

marks

marks

marks

marks

marks

marks

9 Work out the value of $3y - 1$ when $y = 6$ **(1)**

Answer: ....

☐ marks

10 Work out the value of the output when $x = 3$ is input into the expression $x^2 - 1$ **(1)**

Answer: ....

☐ marks

11 Work out the value of $2a + 5$ when $a = -1$
Tick **one** box. **(1)**

☐ **A** 7
☐ **B** -3
☐ **C** -7
☐ **D** 3

☐ marks

12 Work out the value of $2 + 5x$ when $x = -4$ **(1)**

Answer: ....

☐ marks

13 Work out the value of $2a + 5b - 3c$ when $a = 7$, $b = -1$ and $c = 2$ **(1)**

Answer: ....

☐ marks

Make a plan

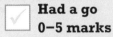 **Had a go** 0–5 marks	**Nearly there** 6–9 marks	**Nailed it!** 10–13 marks	

Make sure you are confident with the basic skills of simplifying algebraic expressions, collecting like terms and substituting into simple formulae. You can then tackle expressions with more than one like term and substitutions with negative numbers.

Well done! Use the hints in the answers to work out where you could have picked up more marks. Remember that if a question asks you to substitute a value into an expression, the answer should be a number – it's a core skill that you need to master.

Congratulations! Keep an eye out for more complicated simplifications. You might need to simplify expressions that have a combination of letters and numbers in them.

MY TOTAL MARKS

Answers on page 100

10 Formulae

You need to be able to write down and use standard mathematical formulae and change the subject of a formula.

 1 A commonly used formula in physics is $F = ma$

My marks

(a) Calculate the value of F when $m = 3$ and $a = 7$ **(1)**

Answer: $F = $ ....

marks

(b) Rearrange the formula to make m the subject. **(1)**

Answer: $m = $ ....

marks

 2 Another formula used in physics is $v = u + at$

(a) Calculate the value of v when $u = 4$, $a = 2$ and $t = 3$ **(1)**

Answer: $v = $ ....

marks

(b) Rearrange the formula to make u the subject. **(1)**

Answer: $u = $ ....

marks

 3 The cost of a taxi is £3 plus 50 pence per mile.

Core skill **(a)** Write down a formula for the cost, £C, of a journey of m miles. **(1)**

Answer: $C = $ ....

marks

(b) Calculate the cost of a journey of 7 miles. **(1)**

Answer: £ ....

marks

(c) Calculate the number of miles travelled if the cost of the journey is £18.50 **(1)**

Answer: .... miles

marks

My
marks

4   Julienne buys x pencils costing 12p each and y pens costing 25p each.

(a) Write down a formula for the total cost, T pence, of the pencils and pens. **(1)**

Answer: ....

marks

(b) Given that Julienne bought 8 pencils and 6 pens, calculate the total cost.
Give your answer in pounds. **(1)**

Answer: £ ....

marks

5   $E = mc^2$
Make c the subject of the formula. **(2)**

$c =$ ....

marks

6   $A = 2b - c$
Which of these is **not** a correct rearrangement of the formula above?
Tick **one** box. **(1)**

☐ **A** $c = 2b - A$

☐ **B** $b = \frac{1}{2}(A + c)$

☐ **C** $b = \frac{c + A}{2}$

☐ **D** $b = \frac{A - c}{2}$

marks

Make a plan

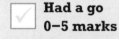 **Had a go**
0–5 marks

You need to be confident with algebra to be able to work with formulae. Practise rearranging and substituting into algebraic expressions.

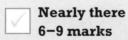 **Nearly there**
6–9 marks

Well done! Practise the core skill of writing a formula using the letters given in the question and include an equals sign. Rearranging formulae is similar to solving equations so you can revise these skills together.

Nailed it!
10–12 marks

Congratulations! Keep an eye out for more complicated formulae that require several steps in their rearrangement. Make sure to use the correct order of operations in these cases.

MY TOTAL MARKS

Answers
on page 100

11 Brackets and factorising

You need to be able to expand and factorise different types of algebraic expression, including quadratic expressions.

1 Expand $3(2a - 5)$ (1)

Answer: ....

 marks

2 Expand $a(3 - a)$ (1)

Answer: ....

 marks

3 Factorise $8x + 6y$ (1)

Answer: ....

 marks

4 Fill in the gaps to complete the factorisation. (2)

$4x^2 - 6x = ... (................... - ....)$

 marks

5 Expand $(x + 4)(x - 3)$ (1)

Core skill

Answer: ....

 marks

6 Work out the correct factorisation of $x^2 - 5x - 14$
Tick **one** box. (1)

Core skill

☐ **A** $(x + 7)(x - 2)$
☐ **B** $(x - 7)(x + 2)$
☐ **C** $(x - 2)(x - 7)$
☐ **D** $(x + 2)(x + 7)$

 marks

7 Fill in the gaps to form a correct mathematical statement. **(1)**

$$x^2 + 8x - 20 = (x\text{.................}\,)\,(x\text{.................})$$

Answer: ....

marks

8 Complete the working to expand and simplify $3(x + 7) + 5(2x - 3)$ **(2)**

$$3(x + 7) + 5(2x - 3) = \text{..........}\,x + 21 + 10x - \text{..........}$$

$$= \text{..........}\,x + \text{..........}$$

Answer: ....

marks

9 The expression $a^2 - b^2$ is mathematically equivalent to which expression?
Tick **one** box. **(1)**

☐ **A** $(a + b)(a + b)$
☐ **B** $(a - b)(a + b)$
☐ **C** $(a - b)(a - b)$
☐ **D** $(a - b)^2$

marks

10 Fill in the gaps to complete the factorisation. **(1)**

$$x^2 - 64 = (x\text{.................}\,)\,(x\text{.................})$$

Answer: ....

marks

Make a plan

☑ **Had a go**
0–4 marks
Make sure you are confident with expanding and factorising single brackets. Then you can tackle the core skills of expanding two sets of brackets and factorising quadratic expressions.

☑ **Nearly there**
5–9 marks
Well done! Remember that if a question asks you to factorise a quadratic expression, you might need two sets of brackets in your answer.

☑ **Nailed it!**
10–12 marks
Congratulations! If you can factorise quadratic expressions then you can solve quadratic equations.

MY TOTAL MARKS

Answers on page 101

12 Definitions and proof

You need to understand the language of mathematics and know how to use algebra to construct mathematical arguments and simple proofs.

1 Choose the correct word from the options below to complete this sentence. **(1)**

identity   equation   expression   inequality

$3(x + 2)$ is an example of an ....

2 Identify which one of the mathematical statements below is an equation.
Tick **one** box. **(1)**

☐ **A** $2x + 3x$
☐ **B** $x \times x = x^2$
☐ **C** $4x + 2 > 2(2x + 1)$
☐ **D** $3x - 1 = 8$

3 Identify the correct description of $7y$ in $4x + 7y - 3$
Tick **one** box. **(1)**

☐ **A** $7y$ is a term
☐ **B** $7y$ is an expression
☐ **C** $7y$ is a formula
☐ **D** $7y$ is a factor

4 Choose the correct word from the options below to complete this sentence. **(1)**

identity   equation   expression   inequality

$x > 3$ is an example of an ....

5 An odd number is written algebraically as $2n + 1$
What is the correct expression for the next odd number?
Tick **one** box. **(1)**

☐ **A** $2n + 3$
☐ **B** $2n + 2$
☐ **C** $3n + 1$
☐ **D** $n + 2$

6 Fill in the gaps to complete the mathematical argument. **(2)**

Core skill $(x + y)^2 = ($...$)($...$)$

$\quad\quad\quad = x^2$ .... $+ y^2$

My marks

☐ marks

☐ marks

☐ marks

☐ marks

☐ marks

☐ marks

7 Fill in the gaps to complete the mathematical argument. **(3)**
The sum of three consecutive even numbers is a multiple of 6

$2n +$ .... $+ (2n + 4) = 6n +$ ....

$= 6($...$)$

The expression in brackets must be a ....

Hence the sum of three consecutive even numbers is a multiple of 6

marks

Make a plan

 Had a go
0–4 marks
Focus on the basic skills of expanding and simplifying algebraic expressions. And make sure you know the difference between an equation, a formula, an expression and an identity.

 Nearly there
5–7 marks
Well done! Use the hints in the answers to work out where you could have picked up more marks. Remember that if a question asks you to complete a mathematical argument, you must show every step in your working.

 Nailed it!
8–10 marks
Congratulations! Keep an eye out for more complicated mathematical arguments. You might need to work with consecutive integers, odd numbers or even numbers.

 MY TOTAL MARKS

Answers on page 102

13 Graphs

  You need to work with coordinates in all four quadrants, solve geometric problems on a coordinate grid and plot straight lines using a table of values.

1 Write down the coordinates of point *A* in the diagram. **(1)**

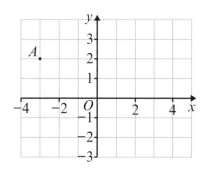

Answer: (...................., ...) | marks

2 Plot the point (2, −1) on the coordinate grid. **(1)**

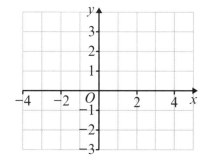

| marks

3 *ABCD* is a rectangle.

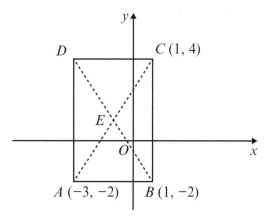

(a) Write down the coordinates of point *D*. **(1)**

Answer: (...................., ...) | marks

E is the centre of the rectangle.

(b) Work out the coordinates of point *E*. **(2)**

Answer: (...................., ...) | marks

4 **(a)** Complete the table of values for the equation $y = 2x - 1$ **(1)**

marks

x	0	1	2
y			

(b) Draw the graph of $y = 2x - 1$ **(1)**

marks

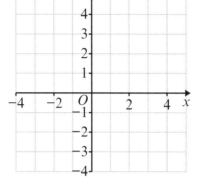

5 Draw and label these graphs on the coordinate grid.

(a) $x = 2$ **(1)**

marks

(b) $y = -1$ **(1)**

marks

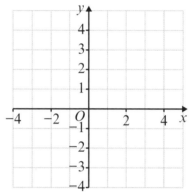

6 **(a)** Complete the table of values for the equation $y = -\frac{1}{3}x + 2$ **(1)**

marks

x	-3	0	3
y			

(b) Draw the graph of $y = -\frac{1}{3}x + 2$ **(1)**

marks

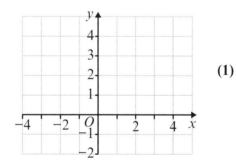

Make a plan

 Had a go
0–4 marks

Make sure you are confident with the basic skills of plotting coordinates on a grid. Then you can tackle the core skill of plotting straight-line graphs using a table of values.

 Nearly there
5–8 marks

Well done! Remember that you should always use a sharp pencil when drawing graphs, and use a ruler to draw any straight lines.

 Nailed it!
9–11 marks

Congratulations! Keep an eye out for more complicated straight-line graphs. And always look at the scale carefully when reading graphs or plotting points.

MY TOTAL MARKS

Answers on page 102

Revision Guide pages 37, 38, 39

14 Straight-line graphs

You can use $y = mx + c$ to find gradients and y-intercepts, and to work out the equations of straight-line graphs.

1 A straight-line graph has equation $y = 5x - 1$

(a) Work out the gradient of the line.
Tick **one** box. **(1)**

- ☐ **A** 5
- ☐ **B** −1
- ☐ **C** 1
- ☐ **D** −5

marks

(b) Work out the coordinates of the y-intercept.
Tick **one** box. **(1)**

- ☐ **A** (0, 1)
- ☐ **B** −1
- ☐ **C** (0, −1)
- ☐ **D** (5, −1)

marks

2 The diagram shows a straight-line graph.

Core skill

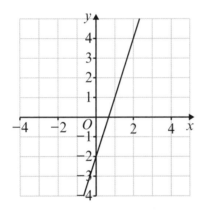

Work out the gradient and y-intercept of the line.

Gradient: .... **(1)**

y-intercept: (...................., ...) **(1)**

marks

3 Write down the equation of the straight line with gradient 4 and y-intercept (0, 3) **(1)**

Answer: ....

marks

4   A straight-line graph has gradient −2 and passes through the point (1, 3)

(a) Calculate the coordinates of the *y*-intercept.   **(1)**

(................., ...)   marks

(b) Write down the equation of the line.   **(1)**

Answer: ....   marks

5   A straight-line graph, *l*, has equation $y = 5x - 3$
Which of these lines is parallel to *l*?
Tick **one** box.   **(1)**

☐ **A** $y = 4x - 3$
☐ **B** $y = 5x + 7$
☐ **C** $y = -5x + 2$
☐ **D** $y = \frac{1}{5}x - 3$ marks

6   A straight line passes through the coordinate points *A*(0, 3) and *B*(1, 5)
Find the equation of the line through *A* and *B*, giving your answer in the
form $y = mx + c$ **(2)**

Gradient: ....

y-intercept: (..................., ...)

Answer: ....   marks

Make a plan

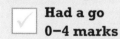 **Had a go**
0–4 marks
Make sure you are confident
plotting points on a coordinate grid.
Remember that if a straight line
has equation $y = mx + c$ then its
gradient is *m* and its *y*-intercept
is (0, *c*).

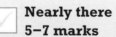 **Nearly there**
5–7 marks
Well done! Use the hints in the
answers to work out where you
could have picked up more marks.
Remember that if a question asks
you to find the equation of a line,
you cannot simply state the gradient
and the *y*-intercept.

Nailed it!
8–10 marks
Congratulations! Keep an eye out
for more complicated straight-line
graphs, and remember that graphs
with negative gradients slope down.
You might need to calculate the
equation of a line with a
fractional gradient.

 MY TOTAL MARKS

Answers on page 103

15 Quadratic and curved graphs

10

You need to be able to plot the graphs of quadratic functions and identify their roots, intercepts and turning points. You also need to know the shapes of other curved graphs.

My marks

1 A graph has equation $y = x^2 + 3x - 2$

Core skill **(a)** Complete the table of values. **(2)**

x	-3	-2	-1	0	1
y	-2	-4		-2	

marks

(b) Draw the graph of $y = x^2 + 3x - 2$ **(2)**

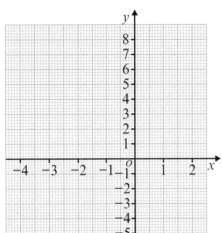

marks

2 Draw lines to match each graph to the correct equation **(2)**

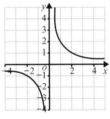 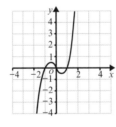 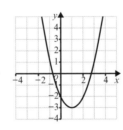 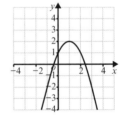

$y = x^3 - x$ $\qquad$ $y = x^2 - 2x - 2$ $\qquad$ $y = \frac{2}{x}$ $\qquad$ $y = 1 + 2x - x^2$

marks

3 This is the graph of $y = x^2 - 5x + 2$

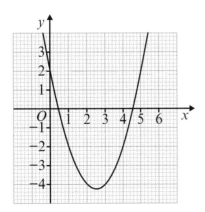

(a) Write down the coordinates of the *y*-intercept. (1)

Answer: (................... , ...)

(b) Write down the values of *x* where the graph crosses the *x*-axis. (2)

Answer: *x* = ... and *x* = ...

(c) Write down the coordinates of the turning point on the graph. (1)

Answer: (................... , ...)

4 Amit draws the graph of $y = x^2 + x - 6$

(a) Identify the points where Amit's graph crosses the *x*-axis.
Tick **one** box. (1)

☐ **A** $(2, 0)$ and $(-3, 0)$
☐ **B** $(2, 0)$ and $(3, 0)$
☐ **C** $(-2, 0)$ and $(3, 0)$
☐ **D** $(-2, 0)$ and $(-3, 0)$

(b) Work out the coordinates of the *y*-intercept on Amit's graph.
Tick **one** box. (1)

☐ **A** $(0, 6)$
☐ **B** $(0, -6)$
☐ **C** $(0, 2)$
☐ **D** $(-6, 0)$

My marks

☐ marks

☐ marks

☐ marks

☐ marks

☐ marks

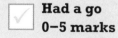
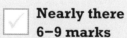
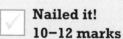

16 Real-life graphs

  You need to be able to use real-life graphs, including conversion graphs, distance–time graphs and velocity–time graphs.

1 The graph shows the relationship between x, the number of miles, and y, the cost in £, of a taxi journey.

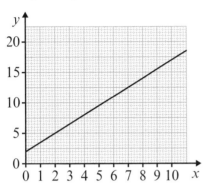

(a) Use the graph to calculate the cost of a journey of 8 miles. **(1)**

Answer: £ ....

marks

(b) Calculate the gradient of the line. **(1)**

Answer: ....

marks

(c) Interpret this value. **(1)**

Answer: ....

marks

(d) Every journey has a fixed charge.
Write down the amount of this fixed charge. **(1)**

Answer: £ ....

marks

2 The graph shows the distance, in km, covered by two cyclists, A and B, during a 4-hour ride.

Core skill

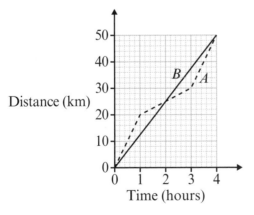

(a) Calculate the speed, in km/h, of cyclist A for the first hour of the ride. **(1)**

Answer: .... km/h

marks

(b) Calculate the speed, in km/h, of cyclist A between 1 and 3 hours. **(1)**

Answer: .... km/h

marks

(c) Write down the distance covered when cyclist *B* overtakes cyclist *A*. **(1)**

Answer: .... km

(d) Is the following statement true or false? **(1)**

The average speed of both cyclists was the same.
☐ True
☐ False

3 This is the velocity–time graph for a car journey.

Velocity (m/s) vertical axis, values 0, 10, 20, 30.
Time (seconds) horizontal axis, values 0 10 20 30 40 50 60 70 80.

Which of the following statements are true?
Tick **two** boxes. **(2)**

☐ **A** The car accelerated during the first 20 seconds.
☐ **B** The car accelerated during the last 30 seconds.
☐ **C** The car travelled at a constant speed between 30 and 50 seconds.
☐ **D** The car accelerated quickest between 0 and 20 seconds.

My marks

☐ marks

☐ marks

☐ marks

Make a plan

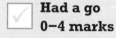 **Had a go
0–4 marks**

Make sure you are confident with the basic skills of reading coordinates and values from graphs. Then you can tackle the core skill of interpreting real-life graphs.

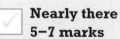 **Nearly there
5–7 marks**

Well done! Remember that if a question asks you to read from a graph, make sure you use the correct units and scales. You can draw lines with a ruler to help you read off a graph and show your working.

**Nailed it!
8–10 marks**

Congratulations! Keep an eye out for more complicated questions about interpreting graphs. Always check the labels on the axes and read the scales carefully.

 MY TOTAL MARKS

Answers on page 104

17 Linear equations

  You need to be able to solve linear equations in one unknown algebraically.

My marks

1 Solve $x - 7 = 8$
Tick **one** box. **(1)**

☐ **A** 1
☐ **B** −1
☐ **C** 15
☐ **D** −15

☐ marks

2 Solve $\frac{x}{4} = 6$ **(1)**

Answer: $x =$ .... ☐ marks

3 Solve the equation $3x - 5 = 1$
Tick **one** box. **(1)**

Core skill

☐ **A** $x = -\frac{4}{3}$
☐ **B** $x = 2$
☐ **C** $x = -2$
☐ **D** $x = \frac{4}{3}$

☐ marks

4 If $3x - 2 = x + 8$, what is the value of x?
Tick **one** box. **(1)**

☐ **A** 3
☐ **B** 4
☐ **C** 5
☐ **D** 6

☐ marks

5 Solve $5x - 6 = 2x + 27$ **(2)**

Answer: $x =$ .... ☐ marks

6 **(a)** Expand $4(3x - 7)$ **(1)**

Answer: .... marks

(b) Hence solve the equation
$4(3x - 7) = 2$ **(2)**

Answer: $x =$ .... marks

 7 Solve $7(2x + 5) = -9$ **(2)**

Answer: $x =$ .... marks

Make a plan

| ✓ | **Had a go** 0–4 marks | ✓ | **Nearly there** 5–8 marks | ✓ | **Nailed it!** 9–11 marks |

 Make sure you are confident with the basic skills of identifying the inverse operations of adding, subtracting, multiplying and dividing. Then you can tackle the core skill of solving linear equations by using these inverse operations.

 Well done! Remember that if a question asks you to solve an equation, get all the x terms on one side and the numbers on the other. Remember that the answer to an equation can be a fraction or a whole number.

 Congratulations! Writing and solving your own equations can be a really good strategy for solving word problems and geometry questions.

 MY TOTAL MARKS

Answers on page 105

Revision Guide pages 47, 49

18 Harder equations

  You need to be able to solve quadratic equations algebraically by factorising. You also need to be able to solve two linear simultaneous equations.

 1 **(a)** Factorise $x^2 - 7x + 6$ **(1)**

Core skill

Answer: $(x$ ....$)(x$ ....$)$

(b) Solve $x^2 - 7x + 6 = 0$ **(1)**

Answer: $x =$ .... or $x =$ ....

2 Solve $x^2 - 12x + 20 = 0$ **(2)**

Answer: $x =$ .... or $x =$ ....

3 Solve $x^2 - 25 = 0$ **(1)**

Answer: $x =$ .... or $x =$ ....

4 **(a)** Factorise $x^2 - 7x$ **(1)**

Answer: ....

(b) Solve $x^2 - 7x = 0$ **(1)**

Answer: $x =$ .... or $x =$ ....

My marks

marks

marks

marks

marks

marks

5 What pair of numbers solve these simultaneous equations?

$$x + 2y = 5$$
$$2x + 3y = 8$$

Tick **one** box. (1)

- [ ] **A** $x = 5, y = 0$
- [ ] **B** $x = -1, y = 3$
- [ ] **C** $x = 3, y = 1$
- [ ] **D** $x = 1, y = 2$

marks

6 Solve these simultaneous equations.

$$2x - 4y = 4$$
$$3x + 2y = 14$$

Core skill

Fill in the gaps below to help you. (3)

$$2x - 4y = 4$$
$$+ \quad \ldots\ldots x + 4y = 28$$
_____

$$\ldots\ldots x = 32$$

$$x = \ldots\ldots\ldots\ldots\ldots$$

Answer: $x = $ .... , $y = $ ....

marks

Make a plan

 Had a go
0–4 marks

Solving quadratic equations is tricky. You need to be really confident factorising linear and quadratic expressions before you tackle this topic.

 Nearly there
5–8 marks

Well done! Remember that if a question asks you to solve a pair of simultaneous equations, you might need to multiply one of the equations first in order to eliminate a variable (letter).

 Nailed it!
9–11 marks

Congratulations! You've nailed this tricky topic. You can always check answers to equations by substituting them back into the original equation.

 MY TOTAL MARKS

Answers on page 106

Revision Guide pages 27, 32, 33, 49

19 Inequalities and using algebra

  You might have to write your own equation to solve a problem. You also need to be able to solve linear inequalities and represent their solution on a number line.

1 **(a)** Solve $x + 7 < 10$ **(1)**

Answer: ....

(b) Represent your solution on this number line. **(1)**

2 Solve the inequality $4x - 7 \geqslant 21$
Tick **one** box. **(1)**

Core skill

☐ **A** $x \leqslant 7$
☐ **B** $x \geqslant 7$
☐ **C** $x \geqslant 3.5$
☐ **D** $x \leqslant 3.5$

3 Write down all the integers that satisfy $15 \leqslant 3x < 24$ **(1)**

Answer: ....

4

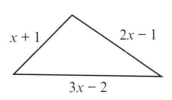

$x + 1$ $2x - 1$
$3x - 2$

(a) Write down a simplified expression for the perimeter of the triangle. **(1)**

Answer: ....

marks

marks

marks

marks

marks

The perimeter of the rectangle is 19 cm.

(b) Calculate the value of x. **(1)**

Answer: $x =$ .... marks

5 2 adult cinema tickets plus 4 child cinema tickets cost £31
4 adult cinema tickets plus 5 child cinema tickets cost £50
Let x represent the cost of an adult ticket and y the cost of a child ticket.

(a) Write down two equations connecting x and y. **(2)**

Answer: ....

.... marks

(b) Which of the following are the prices of the adult and child tickets?
Tick **one** box. **(1)**

☐ **A** Adult: £5.50; Child: £5
☐ **B** Adult: £6.50; Child: £4.50
☐ **C** Adult: £7.50; Child: £4
☐ **D** Adult: £8.50; Child: £3.50

marks

My marks

Make a plan

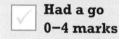 **Had a go**
0–4 marks
If you're struggling with this topic, have another look at your basic algebra skills. These are essential if you're going to master the core skill of solving inequalities.

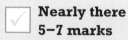 **Nearly there**
5–7 marks
Well done! Use the hints in the answers to work out where you could have picked up more marks. Remember that if a question asks you to solve an inequality, use inverse operations in the same way as you solve an equation.

☑ **Nailed it!**
8–9 marks
Congratulations! Keep an eye out for questions in geometry where you have to form and solve an equation to find, for example, an unknown angle. These applications are common in exam questions.

☐ **MY TOTAL MARKS**

Answers on page 106

Revision Guide pages 34, 35

20 Sequences

You need to be able to continue a given sequence, find missing terms in a sequence, generate terms using a given expression for the nth term and find an expression for the nth term for a given sequence.

1 The first four terms of a sequence are

> 3   5   7   9

Find the next term of the sequence.   **(1)**

Answer: ....

marks

2 The rule for generating a sequence is 'add 3'. The first term of the sequence is 7
Find the third and fourth terms of the sequence.
Tick **one** box.   **(1)**

☐ **A** 10 and 13
☐ **B** 8 and 9
☐ **C** 13 and 16
☐ **D** 16 and 19

marks

3 The nth term of a sequence is $n^2 + 1$
Work out the first three terms of the sequence.   **(1)**

Answer: ....

marks

4 The first five terms of a sequence are

> 5   8   11   14   17

Core skill

Complete the working to find an expression for the nth term.   **(2)**

The difference between the terms is ....

The zero term is ....

Hence the nth term = ... n + ...

marks

5 The rule for generating a sequence is 'add two consecutive terms to get the next term'.
The first four terms are

> 4   5   9   14

Write down the next two terms of this sequence.   **(2)**

Answer: .... and ....

marks

6 Here are the first four terms of a sequence

    3   9   27   81

Find the next term of the sequence. **(1)**

Answer: ....

7 The nth term of a sequence is $5n + 3$

(a) Work out the 9th term of the sequence. **(1)**

Answer: ....

(b) Work out the first term of the sequence that is greater than 61 **(1)**

Answer: ....

8 Here are the first four terms of a sequence

    10   7   4   1

Core skill Work out an expression for the nth term.

Tick **one** box. **(1)**

- [ ] **A** $3n + 7$
- [ ] **B** $n - 3$
- [ ] **C** $13 - 3n$
- [ ] **D** $10 - 3n$

My marks

marks

marks

marks

marks

Make a plan

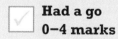 **Had a go**
0–4 marks

Practise spotting patterns in sequences. If you're not confident with nth terms try generating some different sequences from their nth term.

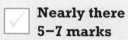 **Nearly there**
5–7 marks

Well done! Use the hints in the answers to work out where you could have picked up more marks. Practise the core skill of finding the nth term by looking at the difference between terms.

Nailed it!
8–11 marks

Congratulations! Keep an eye out for sequences made from patterns – you might need to find an expression for the nth term in practical situations.

 MY TOTAL MARKS

 **Answers on page 107**

21 Units and measuring

  You need to be able to read scales and measure lines and angles accurately.

1

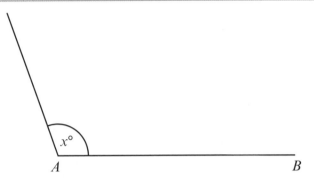

(a) Measure the length of *AB*. **(1)**

Answer: .... cm

(b) Measure the size of the angle *x*°. **(1)**

Answer: .... °

2

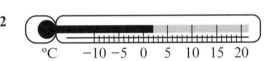

Write down the temperature shown on the thermometer. **(1)**

Answer: .... °C

3 A package is placed on a scale.
What is the weight of the package? **(1)**

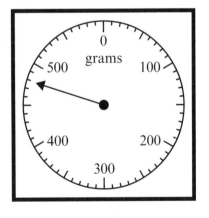

Answer: .... g

4 The speedometer shows the speed of a car.
Estimate the speed in miles per hour (mph). **(1)**

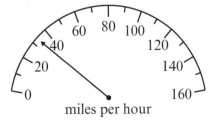

Answer: .... mph

My
marks

5

1000 ml

800

600

400

Write down the reading on the scale in ml. **(1)**

Answer: .... ml

marks

6 **(a)** Change 3 cm to mm. **(1)**

Core skill

Answer: .... mm

marks

(b) Change 560 cm to m. **(1)**

Answer: .... m

marks

7 **(a)** Change 8500 ml to litres. **(1)**

Core skill

Answer: .... litres

marks

(b) Change 7.6 kg to g. **(1)**

Answer: .... g

marks

8 Convert 23 000 mm to metres. **(1)**

Answer: .... m

marks

Make a plan

✓ **Had a go** **0–4 marks**	✓ **Nearly there** **5–8 marks**	✓ **Nailed it!** **9–11 marks**

Try practising measuring lengths and angles and reading scales accurately. Look carefully at the scale to work out the value of any unlabelled markers.

Well done! Make sure you know all the different metric units of length, capacity and mass, and how to convert between them.

Congratulations! Always pay attention to the units when you are working on questions involving speed, distance or time. You might need to convert amounts or give your answer in specific units.

MY TOTAL
MARKS

Answers on page 107

22 Maps and scale drawings

You need to be able to work with standard units when using and interpreting scale factors, scale diagrams, maps and bearings.

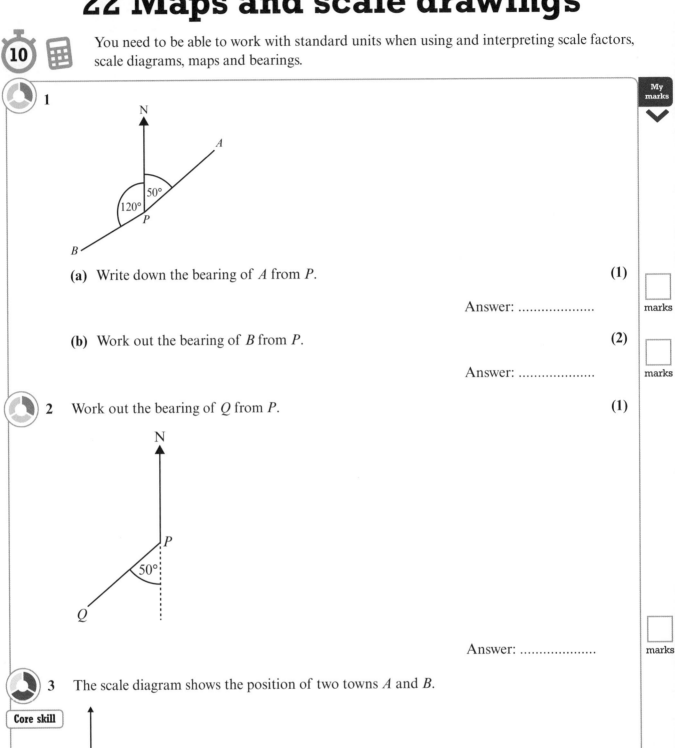

1

(a) Write down the bearing of A from P. **(1)**

Answer: ....

(b) Work out the bearing of B from P. **(2)**

Answer: ....

2 Work out the bearing of Q from P. **(1)**

Answer: ....

3 The scale diagram shows the position of two towns A and B.

Core skill

The scale of the diagram is 1 cm represents 5 km.

(a) Work out the real distance between *A* and *B*. **(1)**

Answer: .... km   marks

(b) Measure the bearing of *B* from *A*. **(1)**

Answer: ....   marks

A town *C* is 30 km from *B* on a bearing of 060°.

(c) On the diagram mark the position of town *C* with a cross (×). Label it *C*. **(2)**   marks

4 A road map has a scale of 1 : 50 000
The length of a road on the map is 8.5 cm.
Work out the actual length of the road in kilometres.
You must show your working. **(2)**

8.5 .... 50 000 = ...

Answer: .... km   marks

5 A car is 4.8 m long. A scale model of the car is made using a scale of 1 : 32
What is the length of the scale model?
Give your answer in centimetres.
You must show your working. **(2)**

Answer: .... cm   marks

Make a plan

☑ **Had a go**
  0–4 marks

Revise your work on bearings and
working with scale drawings and
maps. These are core skills you need
to be able to apply.

☑ **Nearly there**
  5–8 marks

Well done! Use the hints in the
answers to work out where you
could have picked up more marks.
It might help to recap converting
between metric units.

☑ **Nailed it!**
  9–12 marks

Congratulations! Remember to
check that your answers make
sense by thinking about the real-life
context. You can use ratios and scale
to help you answer questions about
similar shapes.

MY TOTAL
MARKS

Answers
on page 108

23 Ratio

 You need to be able to express one quantity as a fraction of another, where the fraction could be less than 1 or greater than 1. You also need to be able to use ratio notation and simplify ratios.

<table>
<tr><td></td><td>My marks</td></tr>
</table>

1 There are 320 red balls and 840 white balls in a ball pool.
Write down in its simplest form

(a) the number of red balls as a fraction of the number of white balls. **(1)**

Answer: .... marks

(b) the number of red balls as a fraction of the total number of balls in the ball pool. **(1)**

Answer: .... marks

2 Which of these ratios is equivalent to $9:4$?
Tick **one** box. **(1)**

☐ **A** $14:20$
☐ **B** $18:13$
☐ **C** $27:12$
☐ **D** $29:24$

marks

3 There are 18 boys and 15 girls in a class.
Write the ratio of boys to girls in its simplest form. **(1)**

Answer: .... marks

4 The height of a room is 2.4 m. The length of the room is 5.7 m.
What is the ratio of the height to the length in the form $1:n$? **(2)**

$2.4:5.7 = \boxed{}:\boxed{}$

Answer: .... marks

My
marks

5 Emma and Matt win some money in a raffle.
They share the money in the ratio 4 : 5
Matt gets £75
How much money did they win in total?
You must show your working. **(3)**

Core skill

£75 = ☐ parts
£☐ = 1 part

Answer: £...................

☐ marks

6 A box contains 56 cards.
Each card is either white or black.
The ratio of the number of white cards to the number of black cards is 1 : 1
7 white cards are removed from the box.
Find the ratio of the number of white cards to the number of black cards now in the box.
Give your answer in its simplest form. **(3)**

At the start:

number of white cards = ...

number of black cards = ...

After 7 white cards removed:

Answer: ....

☐ marks

Make a plan

 Had a go
0–4 marks

Ratios can be tricky. Recap the basic definition of a ratio, and how to divide a quantity in a given ratio. You might also need to revise calculations with fractions.

 Nearly there
5–8 marks

Well done! Use the hints in the answers to work out where you could have picked up more marks. Remember that if a question asks you to write a ratio, the order of the numbers should match the order of the descriptions of the quantities.

 Nailed it!
9–12 marks

Congratulations! Ratio problems are often combined with fractions and percentages. Always read questions carefully so you know which skills to use.

MY TOTAL
MARKS

Answers
on page 109

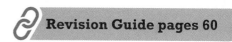

24 Ratio (continued)

10 🧮 You need to be able to solve word problems involving ratios, and understand the relationship between ratios and fractions.

1 In a jar the number of coloured marbles is 3 times the number of clear marbles.
Write down the ratio of the number of clear marbles to the number of coloured marbles in the jar. **(1)**

Core skill

Answer: ....

2 A box of 60 chocolates contains milk chocolates and white chocolates in the ratio 8 : 7
How many milk chocolates are there in the box?
You must show your working. **(2)**

milk chocolates = ☐ parts
white chocolates = ☐ parts
total = ☐ parts

Answer: ....

3 A piece of wood of length 2.1 m is cut into two pieces.
The ratio of the length of the shorter piece to the total length of wood is 3 : 7
What is the length of **each** of the two pieces of wood? **(3)**

2.1 m = ☐ parts
☐ = 1 part

Shorter length: ....

Longer length: ....

My marks

4 Ali and Claire share an amount of money between them in the ratio 3 : 5
Claire receives £15 more than Ali.
How much money did they share? (3)

£15 = ☐ parts
☐ = 1 part

Answer: £ .... marks

5 Ellie, Basim and Saira share £560 between them.
The ratio of Ellie's share to Basim's share is 4 : 5
Saira receives £40 more than Ellie.
Work out how much Basim receives. (3)

Ellie gets ☐ parts
Basim gets ☐ parts
Saira gets ☐ parts + ☐

Total: ....

Answer: £ .... marks

Make a plan

☑ **Had a go**
0–4 marks

Try practising more ratio questions and focus on the core skills of understanding what the different parts of a ratio represent and how ratios relate to fractions.

☑ **Nearly there**
5–8 marks

Well done! Read questions carefully so you are clear about the information given and what you are asked to find. Always check that your answers make sense in the context of the question.

☑ **Nailed it!**
9–12 marks

Congratulations! If you are confident with ratios you will be able to answer questions on proportion and similar shapes more easily.

MY TOTAL MARKS ☐

Answers on page 110

Revision Guide pages 67

25 Ratio and proportion

10 You need to be able to solve problems involving direct proportion, and to understand the relationship between ratio, fractions and proportion.

My marks ⌄

1 Meghan makes some cupcakes for a school fair.

$\frac{2}{5}$ of the cupcakes are chocolate. The rest are vanilla.

Work out the ratio of chocolate cupcakes to vanilla cupcakes in its simplest form.
You must show your working. **(2)**

Fraction that are vanilla = $\frac{\square}{\square}$

Answer: ....

marks

2 12 pencils cost £13.80
How much would 20 pencils cost?
You must show your working. **(2)**

1 pencil = ...

Answer: £ ....

marks

3 On a floor plan of a building, 4 cm represents a length of 5 m.
What length would 10 cm on the floor plan represent?
You must show your working. **(2)**

1 cm = ...

Answer: .... m

marks

4 Becca makes pastry by mixing flour and butter in the ratio 3 : 2

Core skill **(a)** She has 250 g of butter and plenty of flour. What is the maximum weight of pastry she can make?
You must show your working. **(2)**

250 g = $\square$ parts
$\square$ g = 1 part

Answer: .... g

marks

(b) Write an equation to show the linear relationship between the amount of flour, F g in terms of the amount of butter, B g.
You must show your working. **(2)**

$F : B = \square : \square$

so $\dfrac{F}{B} = \dfrac{\square}{\square}$

Answer: ....

$\square$ marks

5 y and x are related by the equation $4y = 5x$
Write down the ratio of $y : x$ **(2)**

Answer: ....

$\square$ marks

Make a plan

☑ **Had a go**
0–4 marks
Try practising basic questions involving proportion, like recipe questions. You can solve a lot of problems by thinking about the weight or cost of one item.

☑ **Nearly there**
5–8 marks
Well done! Always read the question carefully and make sure that you copy any values accurately into your working.

☑ **Nailed it!**
9–12 marks
Congratulations! Being able to work with ratios confidently will help you solve lots of problems involving similar shapes, fractions and percentages.

$\square$
MY TOTAL MARKS

Answers on page 111

26 Percentages

 You need to be able to define percentage as 'number of parts per hundred' and convert between fractions, decimals and percentages. You also need to be able to express one quantity as a percentage of another and compare two quantities using percentages.

My marks ⌄

1 **(a)** Write $\frac{1}{5}$ as a percentage. **(1)**

Core skill

Answer: .... % — marks

(b) Write 0.32 as a percentage. **(1)**

Answer: .... % — marks

(c) Write 82% as a fraction.
Give your answer in its simplest form. **(1)**

Answer: .... — marks

2 By writing them both as percentages, identify which is greater, 0.7 or $\frac{3}{5}$ **(1)**

$0.7 = \boxed{}\%$

$\frac{3}{5} = \boxed{}\%$

Answer: .... — marks

3 Work out 25% of £60 **(1)**

Answer: £ .... — marks

4 Express 36 as a percentage of 48
You must show your working. **(2)**

$$\frac{\boxed{}}{\boxed{}} \times \boxed{}$$

Answer: ....

My marks

☐ marks

5 In a drama class, 40% of the students are males and the rest are females.
Write down the ratio of males to females.
Give your answer in the form $1:n$
You must show your working. **(2)**

Percentage of females = $\boxed{}$ %
Ratio of males to females = $\boxed{}:\boxed{}$

Answer: ....

☐ marks

6 Mike has a bag of coloured counters.

     28% are red
     $\frac{2}{5}$ are white
     0.2 are blue

The remaining counters are yellow.
What percentage of the counters are yellow? **(3)**

$\frac{2}{5} = \boxed{}$%
$0.2 = \boxed{}$%

Answer: ....

☐ marks

Make a plan

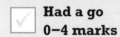 **Had a go**
0–4 marks

Remember that percentages are all about expressing fractions as 'number of parts per hundred'. 5% is the same as 5 parts per hundred, and is the decimal fraction 0.05. Try revising more questions on percentages – this is a core skill you need to be confident with.

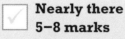 **Nearly there**
5–8 marks

Well done! Use the hints in the answers to work out where you could have picked up more marks. It will help to learn the equivalents of common fractions, decimals and percentages.

 Nailed it!
9–12 marks

Congratulations! If you've mastered basic percentages you will be more confident with harder questions involving percentage change, or combining fractions, percentages and ratio.

☐ MY TOTAL MARKS

Answers on page 112

27 Proportion

  You need to be able to recognise the graphs and equations that represent direct and inverse proportion. You also need to be able to use conversion graphs.

 1 Which sketch graph shows *y* as directly proportional to *x*?
Tick **one** box. (1)

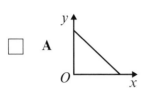

☐ **A**

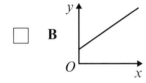

☐ **B**

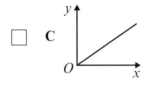

☐ **C**

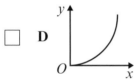

☐ **D**

marks

2 Which equation describes a direct proportion relationship between *y* and *x*?
Tick **one** box. (1)

☐ **A** $y = x + 3$
☐ **B** $y = x^2$
☐ **C** $y = \frac{5}{x}$
☐ **D** $y = 2x$

marks

3 You can use this graph to convert between miles and kilometres.

Core skill

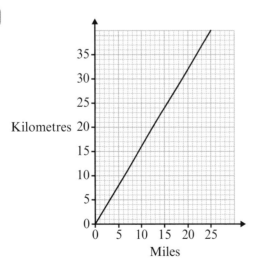

(a) Use the conversion graph to convert 10 miles to kilometres. (1)

Answer: .... km

(b) What does the gradient of the graph represent? (1)

.... per ....

4 Which equation describes an inverse proportion relationship between y and x?
Tick **one** box. (1)

☐ **A** $y = \frac{x}{5}$
☐ **B** $y = 2x^2$
☐ **C** $y = \frac{10}{x}$
☐ **D** $y = 4x$

5 One kilogram of cashew nuts costs £11.79
Paul buys 650 g of cashew nuts.
Work out how much Paul pays. You must show your working. (3)

1 kg = ☐ g
1 g of cashew nuts costs $\frac{\boxed{}}{\boxed{}}$

Answer: £ ....

6 It takes 8 men 9 days to complete a job.

(a) Work out how long it would take 3 men to complete the same job. (3)

1 man would take .... days

Answer: ....

(b) Work out how many men it would take to complete the job in 3 days. (1)

Answer: ....

Make a plan

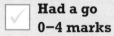 **Had a go**
0–4 marks
Learn the basic shapes of proportion graphs and the equations that show direct and inverse proportion, to give you more confidence with questions like these.

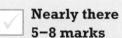 **Nearly there**
5–8 marks
Well done! Use the hints in the answers to work out where you could have picked up more marks. Remember that for inverse proportion, one quantity gets smaller when the other one gets larger.

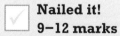 **Nailed it!**
9–12 marks
Congratulations! If you have time in your exam you should check your answers to word problems. Read the question again, and check that your final answer makes sense.

MY TOTAL MARKS

Answers on page 112

28 Compound measures

You need to be able to work confidently with compound units such as speed, rates of pay, unit pricing, density and pressure.

10

1 A train travels at a constant speed of 125 miles per hour for 30 minutes.
Work out the distance travelled.

Core skill

You must show your working. **(2)**

30 minutes = $\dfrac{\square}{\square}$ hour

distance = ... × ....

Answer: .... miles

marks

2 The mass of a brick is 1.5 kg. The volume is $0.0008\,m^3$.
Work out the density of the brick in kg/m^3.
You must show your working. **(2)**

density = $\dfrac{....................}{....................}$ = $\dfrac{....................}{....................}$

Answer: .... kg/m^3

marks

3 The average speed of a cyclist is 10 m/s.
Convert 10 m/s to km/h.
You must show your working. **(2)**

10 m/s = ... m/h

= .... km/h

Answer: .... km/h

marks

4 The water from a garden hose flows at a rate of 75 litres per minute.
A children's paddling pool holds 530 litres of water.
How long will it take to fill the paddling pool in minutes and seconds?
You must show your working. **(2)**

Time = $\boxed{}$ ÷ $\boxed{}$

= $\boxed{}$

Answer: .... minutes .... seconds

marks

My marks

5 Cora travels 63 km in 2 hours 15 minutes.
Work out her average speed in km/h.
You must show your working. (2)

2 hours 15 minutes = ☐ hours

$$\text{average speed} = \frac{\text{....................}}{\text{....................}}$$

Answer: .... km/h

☐ marks

6 A box exerts a force of 120 newtons on a table.
The pressure on the table is 25 newtons/m^2.
Calculate the area of the box that is in contact with the table.
You must show your working. (2)

$p = \dfrac{F}{A}$
p = pressure
F = force
A = area

Substituting values of F and p into the equation: $\boxed{} = \dfrac{\boxed{}}{A}$

Rearranging the equation: $A = \dfrac{\boxed{}}{\boxed{}}$

Answer: ....

☐ marks

Make a plan

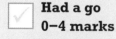 **Had a go**
0–4 marks
Revise formulae and substituting into algebraic expressions.
Then learn the formula triangles for speed and density.

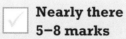 **Nearly there**
5–8 marks
Well done! You can use units to help you work out what calculations to do. For example, if the units are m/s you have to divide metres by seconds.

 Nailed it!
9–12 marks
Congratulations! Watch out for tricky compound measure questions where you have to convert units before calculating. And always check that your final answer makes sense.

MY TOTAL MARKS

Answers on page 113

29 Percentage change

You need to be able to answer questions involving percentage increase or decrease. You might also have to answer questions involving repeated percentage change, like compound interest.

1 A clothes company reduces its prices by 15% in a sale.

Core skill

(a) A jumper normally costs £60
Work out the sale price of the jumper.
You must show your working. **(2)**

Reduction in price = $\dfrac{\boxed{}}{\boxed{}} \times \boxed{}$

Sale price =

Answer: £ .... | marks

(b) A jumper costs £44 in the sale.
Which is the correct calculation to work out the normal price of the jumper?
Tick **one** box. **(1)**

☐ **A** 44 × 1.15
☐ **B** 44 ÷ 1.15
☐ **C** 44 × 0.85
☐ **D** 44 ÷ 0.85

| marks

2 Write down the multipliers for

(a) an increase of 9.5% **(1)**

Answer: .... | marks

(b) a decrease of 12%. **(1)**

Answer: .... | marks

3 Wayne sells radios.
In one week he sells 96 radios.
The next week he sells 132 radios.
Work out the percentage increase in the number of radios he sells.
You must show your working. **(2)**

Actual increase = $\boxed{} - \boxed{}$

Percentage increase = $\dfrac{\text{....................}}{\text{....................}} \times 100$

Answer: .... % | marks

4 Gavin invests £600 for 4 years in a bank account.
The account pays simple interest at a rate of 2.4% per year.
Work out the total amount of interest Gavin has received at the end of 4 years.
You must show your working. **(3)**

Interest for 1 year = $\dfrac{\boxed{}}{\boxed{}} \times \boxed{}$

Interest for 4 years = $4 \times \boxed{}$

Answer: £ ....

☐ marks

5 £500 is invested at 3% per annum compound interest.

(a) Write down the multiplier you need to use to work out the total amount in the account after 1 year. **(1)**

Answer: ....

☐ marks

The £500 is invested for 4 years.

(b) Work out the total amount in the account after 4 years. **(2)**

Total amount = $500 \times \boxed{}^{\boxed{}}$

Answer: £ ....

☐ marks

Make a plan

☑ **Had a go**
0–5 marks

Revise basic percentages and finding percentages of amounts. You can work out a percentage increase by finding the percentage of the amount and adding it on.

☑ **Nearly there**
6–9 marks

Well done! Revise converting percentage increases and decreases into multipliers. If you can do this confidently then reverse percentages are much easier.

☑ **Nailed it!**
10–13 marks

Congratulations! Watch out for words like growth, decay or depreciation. These are clues you might have to do a repeated percentage change.

☐ **MY TOTAL MARKS**

Answers on page 114

30 2-D shapes

You need to know the properties and definitions of special types of quadrilaterals and triangles, understand the vocabulary of the circle and solve geometrical problems on coordinate axes.

1 (a) Write 'acute', 'obtuse' or 'reflex' to complete the description of the angle shown. **(1)**

The angle is ....

(b) Name the triangle shown. **(1)**

The triangle is ....

2 State the name of this quadrilateral. **(1)**

Core skill

Answer: ....

3

(a) Identify what is indicated by **X** in the diagram above.
Tick **one** box. **(1)**

☐ **A** Diameter
☐ **B** Chord
☐ **C** Radius
☐ **D** Circumference

(b) Identify what is indicated by **Y** in the diagram above. **(1)**

Answer: ....

My marks

☐ marks

☐ marks

☐ marks

☐ marks

☐ marks

4 *A*, *B* and *C* are three vertices of a quadrilateral *ABCD*.

Write down the coordinates of *D* if the quadrilateral is

(a) a kite   **(1)**

Answer: (.................., ...)   marks

(b) a parallelogram.   **(1)**

Answer: (.................., ...)   marks

Jemima plots *D* at point (2, 6).

(c) Write down the name of the quadrilateral that Jemima has drawn.   **(1)**

Answer: ....   marks

5 Are the following statements true or false?

(a) All squares are rectangles.   **(1)**
True ☐
False ☐   marks

(b) All isosceles triangles are equilateral triangles.   **(1)**
True ☐
False ☐   marks

Make a plan

| ☑ | **Had a go**
0–4 marks | ☑ | **Nearly there**
5–7 marks | ☑ | **Nailed it!**
8–10 marks |

Make sure that you understand the basic vocabulary of shapes. Then you can tackle questions where you have to name parts of shapes and describe shapes from given information.

Well done! Use the hints in the answers to work out where you could have picked up more marks. Remember that if a question asks you to write down the name of a shape, or part of a shape, you should use the correct vocabulary.

Congratulations! Keep an eye out for questions involving the angle or symmetry properties of triangles and quadrilaterals.

MY TOTAL MARKS ☐

Answers on page 115

31 Constructions

You need to be able to use standard ruler and compass constructions and construct loci.

1 Construct the perpendicular bisector of this line. **(1)**

marks

2 Construct the bisector of this angle. **(1)**

marks

3 Construct a triangle with sides 8 cm, 6 cm and 5 cm. **(2)**

8 cm

marks

4 Construct the locus of points that are within 5 cm of point *A* and 4 cm of point *B*. **(2)**

Core skill

A

B

marks

5 *ABCD* represents a rectangular garden. *AB* = 10 m and *BC* = 18 m.
1 cm in the diagram represents 2 m.

A _____ D

B _____ C

Tim, a keen gardener, wants to plant a crop of broad beans within 8 m of *C* and within 6 m
of side *AD*.
Construct the region in which Tim should plant his broad beans. **(3)**

marks

6 Is the following statement true or false? Give a reason for your answer. **(2)**

It is possible to construct a triangle with side lengths 10 cm, 6 cm and 3 cm.
True ☐
False ☐

Reason: ....

....

marks

Make a plan

☑ **Had a go** **0–4 marks**	☑ **Nearly there** **5–8 marks**	☑ **Nailed it!** **9–11 marks**
Make sure that you can accurately use a ruler and a pair of compasses. Then you can tackle the core skill of using constructions in loci problems.	Well done! Use the hints in the answers to work out where you could have picked up more marks. Remember that if a question asks you to construct something, you should show all of your construction lines.	Congratulations! Keep an eye out for loci questions involving more than two different loci. Check the question to make sure you have shaded the correct region.

MY TOTAL MARKS ☐

Answers on page 115

32 Solving angle problems

  You need to be able to apply the properties of angles to calculate the size of unknown angles.

 1 Write down the size of angle *x* in the diagram.
Give a reason for your answer. **(2)**

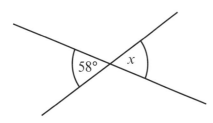

$x =$ .... °

Reason: ....

My marks

☐ marks

 2 Calculate the size of angle *y* in the diagram below.
Give a reason for your answer. **(2)**

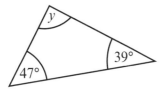

$y =$ .... °

Reason: .... marks ☐

 3 Work out the size of the missing angles in the diagram below.
Give a reason for your answer. **(4)**

Core skill

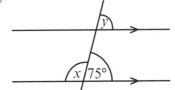

$x =$ .... °

Reason: ....

$y =$ .... °

Reason: .... mark ☐

4 A regular octagon is shown below.

Core skill

(a) Write down the size of one exterior angle. **(1)**

Answer: .... °

☐ marks

(b) Calculate the size of one interior angle. **(1)**

Answer: .... °

☐ marks

5 The three angles in a triangle are $2x$, $3x$ and $4x$.
Calculate x. **(2)**

$x = $ ....

☐ marks

Make a plan

☑ **Had a go**
0–4 marks

Learn the basic rules about angles
in triangles, angles on straight lines
and angles at a point. When you're
confident with these, revise angles in
parallel lines.

☑ **Nearly there**
5–8 marks

Well done! Revise angles in
regular polygons. And remember
that if a question asks you to give a
reason for your answer, you must use
the correct mathematical language.
You can't say 'F-angles' or
'Z-angles'.

☑ **Nailed it!**
9–12 marks

Congratulations! Watch out for
angle problems that involve algebra.
You might need to form and solve
your own equation to find a
missing angle.

**MY TOTAL
MARKS**

**Answers
on page 116**

Revision Guide pages 109, 110, 111

33 Similar and congruent shapes

You need to be able to use similarity and the rules for congruence to find sides and angles.

10

1 Which of the following is **not** a correct criterion for congruence?
Tick **one** box. **(1)**

- [ ] **A** RHS
- [ ] **B** SSS
- [ ] **C** SAS
- [ ] **D** SSA

My marks

marks

2 Which two shapes are congruent? **(1)**

A   B   C   D   E   F

Answer: .... and ....   marks

3

Core skill

22.5 cm   37.5 cm

9 cm

Triangle XYZ is similar to triangle ABC.
$AB = 22.5\,cm$
$BC = 37.5\,cm$
$XY = 9\,cm$

(a) Work out the ratio of the lengths of triangle XYZ to the lengths of triangle ABC in its simplest form. **(1)**

Answer: ....   marks

(b) Work out the length of YZ. **(1)**

.... cm   marks

4 Triangles *ABC* and *DEF* are similar.

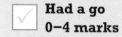

AB = 8 cm, *DE* = 6 cm and *BC* = 12 cm.

(a) Write down the angle that corresponds to angle *A*. **(1)**

Answer: ....

marks

(b) Calculate the length *EF*. **(1)**

Answer: .... cm

marks

5 Here are four statements. Two of the statements are true.
Identify the correct statements.
Tick **two** boxes. **(2)**

☐ **A** All squares are similar.
☐ **B** All rectangles are similar.
☐ **C** All isosceles triangles are similar.
☐ **D** All equilateral triangles are similar.

marks

6 Two rectangles are mathematically similar.
Rectangle **A** has side lengths 10 cm and 14 cm.
Rectangle **B** has one side of length 8 cm.
Find, correct to 3 significant figures, the two possible lengths of the second side
of rectangle **B**. **(2)**

Answer: .... cm or .... cm

marks

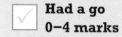
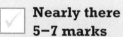

34 Transformations

  You need to be able to describe and construct transformations.

1 Write down the vector that translates shape **A** onto shape **B**. (2)

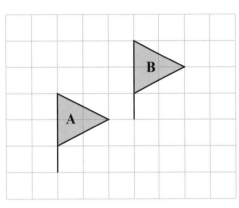

Vector: $\begin{pmatrix} \dots \\ \dots \end{pmatrix}$

☐ marks

2

Core skill

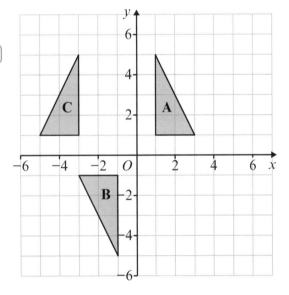

Describe the single transformation that maps:

(a) triangle **A** onto triangle **B** (2)

....

☐ marks

(b) triangle **A** onto triangle **C**. (2)

....

☐ marks

My marks

67

3

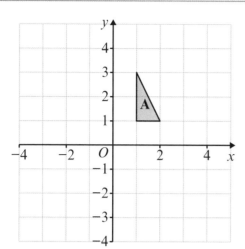

Triangle **B** is a translation of triangle **A** with vector $\begin{pmatrix} -3 \\ -1 \end{pmatrix}$.

Triangle **C** is a rotation of triangle **A** through 90° clockwise about (0, 0).

Draw and label triangles **B** and **C**.　　　　　　　　　　　　　　　　**(2)** marks

4 Enlarge the triangle below, scale factor $\frac{1}{2}$, using (0, 1) as the centre of enlargement.　　**(2)**

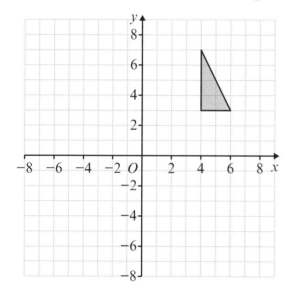

marks

Make a plan

 Had a go
0–4 marks

Make sure that you understand the vocabulary of transformations. Then you can tackle the core skill of describing transformations.

 Nearly there
5–7 marks

Well done! Remember that if a question asks you to describe a transformation, you must name the type of transformation and give enough detail to fully describe it.

 Nailed it!
8–10 marks

Congratulations! Keep an eye out for questions where you have to rotate shapes about points other than (0, 0).

MY TOTAL MARKS

Answers
on page 117

35 Representing 3-D shapes

You need to be able to identify properties of 3-D shapes and draw plans and elevations.

1 Fill in the gaps in the sentence below. **(3)**

A square-based pyramid has .... faces, ... edges and .... vertices.

2 Which one of the following is **not** a possible shape for a face of a triangular prism?
Tick **one** box. **(1)**

☐ **A** Square
☐ **B** Rectangle
☐ **C** Triangle
☐ **D** Trapezium

3 Write the name of each 3-D shape.

(a)

(1)

Answer: ....

(b)

(1)

Answer: ....

(c)

(1)

Answer: ....

4 Which of the following nets will make a cube?
Tick **one** box. **(1)**

☐ **A**

☐ **B**

☐ **C**

☐ **D**

My marks

☐ marks

☐ marks

☐ marks

☐ marks

☐ marks

☐ marks

5 The plan, front elevation and side elevation of a 3-D shape are shown below.

Core skill

Plan   Front elevation   Side elevation

What is the name of the 3-D shape?   (1)

Answer: ....

My
marks

marks

6

Front

Side

Using the grid below, draw the side elevation, front elevation and plan of this object.   (3)

Side elevation   Front elevation

Plan

marks

Make a plan

| ✓ **Had a go** 0–4 marks | ✓ **Nearly there** 5–8 marks | ✓ **Nailed it!** 9–12 marks |

Had a go
0–4 marks

Revise the names of 3-D shapes and practise picturing them from the top and sides to work out their plans and elevations.

Nearly there
5–8 marks

Well done! Use the hints in the answers to work out where you could have picked up more marks. Remember that if a question asks you to draw a plan or elevation, you should mark clearly any changes in depth.

Nailed it!
9–12 marks

Congratulations! Remember to use a sharp pencil when drawing plans and elevations, and always draw straight lines with a ruler.

MY TOTAL
MARKS

Answers
on page 118

36 Lengths and areas

10 🔢 You need to be able to use standard units of length, understand scales and use bearings, and know and apply formulae to calculate perimeters and areas.

1 A square has side length 7 cm.

    (a) Work out the perimeter of the square **(1)**

                        Answer: .... cm

    (b) Work out the area of the square. **(1)**

                        Answer: .... cm^2

2 The triangle shown below has base 9 cm and perpendicular height 6 cm.

Core skill

6 cm

9 cm

    Calculate the area of the triangle. **(1)**

                        Answer: .... cm^2

3 A circle has radius 3 cm.

Core skill   **(a)** Work out the circumference of the circle **(1)**

                        Answer: .... cm

    (b) Work out the area of the circle. **(1)**

                        Answer: .... cm^2

4 A circle has an area of 81π cm^2.
Calculate the diameter of the circle. **(1)**

                        Answer: .... cm

5 A map has a scale of 1 : 15 000
Calculate, in km, the distance in real life represented by a distance of 9 cm on the map. **(1)**

                        Answer: .... km

6 The bearing of Coventry from Stratford-upon-Avon is 031°.
Find the bearing of Stratford-upon-Avon from Coventry. **(1)**

                        Answer: .... °

My marks

My marks

7 The sector shown has a radius of 7 cm and the angle at the centre is 110°.

110°

7 cm

Giving your answers to 3 significant figures,

(a) calculate the area of the sector **(1)**

Answer: .... cm² ☐ marks

(b) calculate the perimeter of the sector. **(1)**

Answer: .... cm ☐ marks

8 Identify the area equivalent to 10 m².
Tick **one** box. **(1)**

☐ **A** 10 000 cm²
☐ **B** 100 000 cm²
☐ **C** 1 000 000 cm²
☐ **D** 1000 cm²

☐ marks

9 The diagram shows a parallelogram joined to a trapezium. The parallelogram and the trapezium have the same perpendicular height.

Calculate the area of this shape. **(2)**

21 cm

24 cm   17 cm

Answer: .... cm² ☐ marks

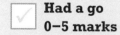

37 Volumes and surface areas

10 You need to know how to calculate volumes and surface areas of 3-D shapes and apply the concept of similarity to 3-D shapes.

1 A cuboid has side lengths 4 cm, 6 cm and 8 cm.
Calculate the volume of the cuboid. **(1)**

Answer: .... cm^3

2 The formula for the volume of a sphere is $V = \frac{4}{3}\pi r^3$.
Calculate, to 3 significant figures, the volume of a sphere with radius 7 cm. **(1)**

Answer: .... cm^3

3 The formula for the volume of a cone is $V = \frac{1}{3}\pi r^2 h$.
Calculate the volume of a cone with base radius 6 cm and perpendicular height 8 cm.
Give your answer as an exact multiple of π. **(1)**

Answer: .... cm^3

4 The formula for the surface area of a sphere is $A = 4\pi r^2$.
Calculate the surface area of a sphere of diameter 10 cm.
Tick **one** box. **(1)**

☐ **A** 400π
☐ **B** 200π
☐ **C** 20π
☐ **D** 100π

5 The prism shown below has a cross-section in the shape of a trapezium.

Core skill

5 cm

6 cm

8 cm

18 cm

Calculate the volume of the prism. **(2)**

Area of cross-section: .... cm^2

Volume: .... cm^3

My marks

marks

marks

marks

marks

marks

6 A cylinder has a volume of $180\pi\,\mathrm{cm}^3$ and a base radius of $1.5\,\mathrm{cm}$.
Calculate the height of the cylinder. **(2)**

Answer: .... cm

marks

 7 Two similar cones have base diameters $18\,\mathrm{cm}$ and $30\,\mathrm{cm}$ respectively.

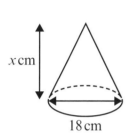 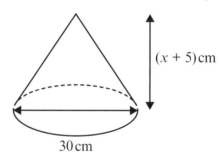

The height of the smaller cone is $x\,\mathrm{cm}$ and the height of the larger cone is $(x + 5)\,\mathrm{cm}$.
Calculate the value of x. **(2)**

$x = $ ....

marks

Make a plan

MY TOTAL MARKS

Answers on page 119

38 Right-angled triangles

You need to know and be able to use Pythagoras' theorem and the trigonometric ratios. You also need to know the exact values of the sine, cosine and tangent of some angles.

1 Calculate the value of x in this right-angled triangle. **(1)**

Core skill

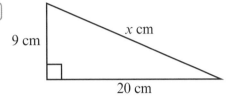

9 cm

x cm

20 cm

Answer: x = ...

2 Calculate the value of x in this right-angled triangle. **(1)**

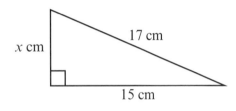

17 cm

x cm

15 cm

Answer: x = ...

3 Calculate the size of angle x in this right-angled triangle. **(1)**

Core skill

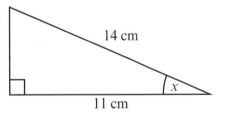

14 cm

x

11 cm

Answer: x = ... °

4 Calculate the value of x in this right-angled triangle. **(1)**

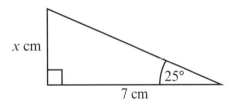

x cm

25°

7 cm

Answer: x = ...

5 One pair of these stated ratios both have value $\frac{\sqrt{3}}{2}$. Identify which pair.
Tick **one** box. **(1)**

    □ **A** sin 30° and cos 60°
    □ **B** sin 60° and cos 30°
    □ **C** sin 60° and cos 60°
    □ **D** sin 30° and cos 30°

My marks

marks

marks

marks

marks

marks

6 The diagram shows a right-angled isosceles triangle.

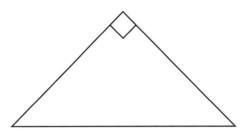

Use the diagram to explain why tan 45° = 1. **(2)**

Explanation: ....

....

marks

7 Calculate the value of x in the diagram below. **(3)**

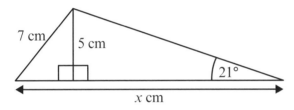

$x =$ ....

marks

Make a plan

 Had a go
0–4 marks

Make sure that you are confident with squaring and taking the square root. Then you can tackle the core skill of applying Pythagoras' theorem to right-angled triangles.

 Nearly there
5–7 marks

Well done! Remember that if a question asks you to find an angle, in a right-angled triangle you must use one of the trigonometric ratios. Label the sides and angles of the triangle and then use SOHCAHTOA to help you decide which ratio to use.

 Nailed it!
8–10 marks

Congratulations! Always check that your final answer makes sense. The diagram won't be to scale but any lengths or angles you find should look about right.

MY TOTAL MARKS

Answers
on page 120

76

39 Vectors

  You need to be able to describe translations using vectors, add or subtract vectors, or multiply a vector by a number.

 1 Draw the vector $\begin{pmatrix} 3 \\ 2 \end{pmatrix}$ on the grid below. **(1)**

☐ marks

 2

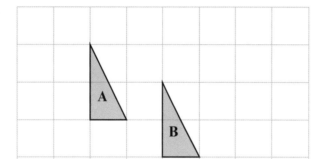

Write down the vector that maps shape **A** onto shape **B**. **(1)**

Answer: .... ☐ marks

 3 $\mathbf{a} = \begin{pmatrix} 4 \\ 2 \end{pmatrix}$, $\mathbf{b} = \begin{pmatrix} 3 \\ -1 \end{pmatrix}$ and $\mathbf{c} = \begin{pmatrix} -2 \\ 6 \end{pmatrix}$

Core skill Calculate the following vectors.

(a) $\mathbf{a} + \mathbf{b}$ **(1)**

Answer: .... ☐ marks

(b) $\mathbf{b} + \mathbf{c}$ **(1)**

Answer: .... ☐ marks

My marks

(c) $3\mathbf{b}$ (1)

Answer: .... marks

(d) $\mathbf{c} - \mathbf{b}$ (1)

Answer: .... marks

(e) $4\mathbf{a} + 3\mathbf{b} - \mathbf{c}$ (2)

Answer: .... marks

4 $\mathbf{b} = \begin{pmatrix} 8 \\ -3 \end{pmatrix}$ and $\mathbf{c} = \begin{pmatrix} -2 \\ 5 \end{pmatrix}$

Find a vector $\mathbf{a}$ such that $2\mathbf{a} + 3\mathbf{b} = 4\mathbf{c}$ (3)

$\mathbf{a} = $ .... marks

 Make a plan

 Had a go
0–4 marks

Revise adding and subtracting negative numbers. This will make adding and subtracting vectors much easier.

Nearly there
5–8 marks

Well done! Remember that if a question asks you to calculate the result of adding, subtracting or multiplying vectors, you must give your answer as a single vector.

 Nailed it!
9–11 marks

Congratulations! Being confident with vectors will help you to describe translations on coordinate grids.

 MY TOTAL MARKS

 Answers on page 121

40 Probability

 You need to understand probabilities, and work out the probability that something will happen. You also need to use frequency tables and trees, and to know that the probabilities of all possible outcomes of an event add up to 1.

1 Here is a fair four-sided spinner.
The spinner can land on blue or on red or on green.

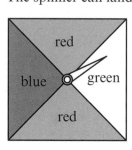

Sylvie spins the spinner once.

(a) On the probability scale, mark with a cross (×) the probability that the spinner will land on green. **(1)**

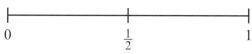

marks

(b) On the probability scale, mark with a cross (×) the probability that the spinner will **not** land on blue. **(1)**

marks

2 There are some red pens, some blue pens and some green pens in a box.
There are   4 red pens
                 8 blue pens
        and   12 green pens in the box.
Jack takes a pen from the box at random.

 Core skill

(a) Write down the probability that Jack takes a blue pen from the box. **(1)**

Total number of pens = ...

Probability (blue pen) = $\dfrac{\square}{\square}$

marks

Jack takes two pens at random from the box.

(b) Write down all the possible combinations of colours of two pens that Jack can take. **(2)**

marks

3 The table shows the probabilities that a biased dice will land on 1, on 2, on 3, on 4 and on 5

Number on dice	1	2	3	4	5	6
Probability	0.14	0.08	0.16	0.12	0.19	

(a) Work out the probability the dice will land on 6.
You must show your working. **(2)**

P(6) = ... – ....

Answer: ....

☐ marks

(b) Bradley rolls the biased dice 200 times.
Work out an estimate for the total number of times the dice will land on 3 **(1)**

Answer: ....

☐ marks

4 There are 300 students in Year 11.
120 of these are girls.
40 of the students are **not** going on to Year 12.
155 of the boys are going on to Year 12.

(a) Use this information to complete the frequency tree. You must show your working. **(3)**

Number of boys = ...

Number of boys **not** going to

Year 12 = ...

☐ marks

Frequency tree: 300 → girls (120) → going to year 12 ◯, not going to year 12 ◯; 300 → boys ◯ → going to year 12 (155), not going to year 12 ◯

One of the students is picked at random.

(b) Write down the probability that this student is a girl **not** going on to Year 12. **(1)**

Answer: ....

☐ marks

Make a plan

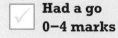 **Had a go**
0–4 marks
Practise identifying the frequencies of different outcomes in simple probability questions before tackling the core skill of working out their probabilities. It might help to revise working with fractions.

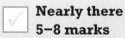 **Nearly there**
5–8 marks
Well done! Use the hints in the answers to work out where you could have picked up more marks. Read questions carefully to be sure you know what you're being asked to work out.

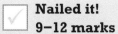 **Nailed it!**
9–12 marks
Congratulations! Watch out if you have to find a probability using information given in a table or diagram. Read off the number of successful outcomes and the total number of possible outcomes carefully.

 MY TOTAL MARKS

 **Answers on page 121**

Revision Guide pages 129, 130, 131, 132

41 Experimental probability

  You need to be able to calculate probabilities based on experiments and data. You should understand that the more trials there are, the more accurate the experimental probabilities will be.

My marks

 1 A class of 24 students complete a test. The test is marked out of 60 The scores are recorded below.

| 36 | 12 | 21 | 48 | 54 | 17 | 38 | 52 | 10 | 45 | 37 | 28 |
| 25 | 39 | 44 | 27 | 40 | 32 | 27 | 18 | 42 | 39 | 51 | 16 |

(a) Complete the tally and frequency columns in the chart below. **(2)**

Score	Tally	Frequency
1–10		
11–20		
21–30		
31–40		
41–50		
51–60		

(b) The pass mark for the test is 41 marks. How many students passed the test? **(1)**

Answer: ....

(c) A student is picked at random. What is the probability they scored 30 marks or less? **(2)**

$$P(\text{scored 30 or less}) = \frac{\Box}{\Box}$$

 2 Kate plays a game with two sets of cards.

Set 1 [1] [3] [5] [7] [9]

Set 2 [2] [4] [6] [8]

Kate takes one card at random from each set. She adds the numbers to get the total score.

(a) Complete the sample space diagram to show all the possible scores. **(1)**

		Set 1				
		1	3	5	7	9
Set 2	2	3	5	7	9	11
	4	5	7	9		
	6					
	8					

(b) What is the probability that Kate's total score will be greater than 12? **(2)**

$$P(\text{score greater than 12}) = \frac{\Box}{\Box}$$

3 Four friends each throw a dice a number of times.

The table shows the number of trials and the number of times the dice landed on 6 for each friend.

	Ali	Ben	Caz	Dom
Number of trials	20	40	100	60
Number of 6s	3	8	25	12

Core skill

(a) Use all the results in the table to work out an estimate for the probability that the dice will land on 6 **(2)**

Total number of trials = ...

Total number of 6s = ...

Estimated probability = $\dfrac{\text{....................}}{\text{....................}}$

Answer: .... | marks

(b) Write down the theoretical probability of rolling a 6 on a fair dice. **(1)**

Theoretical probability = $\dfrac{\square}{\square}$ | marks

(c) Assuming the dice is fair, complete the following statement. **(1)**

The friend whose results will give the best estimate for the theoretical probability is

.... because this friend had the .... number of .... | marks

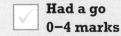
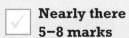
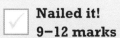

42 Venn diagrams

  You need to be able to draw and interpret Venn diagrams, including the use of set notation, and use them to calculate probabilities.

 1 ξ = the integers from 1 to 16
    A = factors of 12
    B = factors of 16
    Complete the Venn diagram for this information. **(3)**

My marks

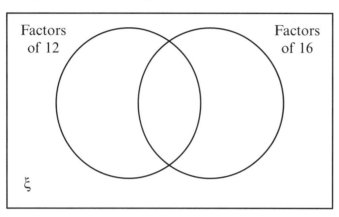

☐ marks

2 There are 80 students at a college.
    25 students study both Maths and English.
    18 students study Maths but not English.
    A total of 52 students study English.

    (a) Complete the Venn diagram for this information. **(3)**

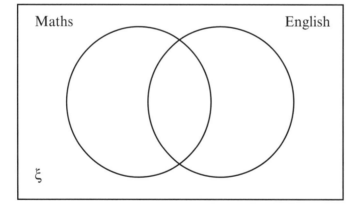

☐ marks

One of the students is picked at random.

    (b) Write down the probability that this student studies neither Maths nor English. **(1)**

Answer: ....

☐ marks

3 Here is a Venn diagram.

Core skill

A 24 3 5 10 12 8 22 B ξ 9 11 23 18

(a) How many numbers are in the universal set ξ? **(1)**

Answer: .... marks

(b) Write down the numbers that are in set

(i) $A \cup B$ **(1)**

Answer: .... marks

(ii) $A \cap B$. **(1)**

Answer: .... marks

One of the numbers in the diagram is picked at random.

(c) Find the probability that the number is in set A'. **(2)**

P(number is in set A') = $\dfrac{\square}{\square}$

Answer: .... marks

Make a plan

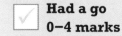 **Had a go**
0–4 marks

Venn diagrams are a useful way of sorting data. Practise working with Venn diagrams and set notation so you feel confident answering probability questions based on them.

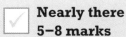 **Nearly there**
5–8 marks

Well done! Use the hints in the answers to work out where you could have picked up more marks. You need to learn the meaning of the symbols used in set notation to be able to answer questions based on Venn diagrams.

 Nailed it!
9–12 marks

Congratulations! If you're drawing a Venn diagram you can check your answer by making sure the frequencies on the Venn diagram add up to the total frequency.

MY TOTAL
MARKS

Answers
on page 123

43 Combined events

⏱ **10** 🖩 You need to be able to calculate the probabilities of combined events, including using tree diagrams.

1 Which of these pairs of events is not independent?
Tick **one** box. **(1)**

☐ **A** Rolling a 6 on a dice, then rolling another 6.

☐ **B** Picking a red sweet from a bag of coloured sweets, putting it back, then picking another red sweet.

☐ **C** Picking a milk chocolate from a box of milk and dark chocolates, eating it, then picking another milk chocolate.

☐ **D** Picking a shirt from a wardrobe at random, then picking a tie at random.

☐ marks

2 Event A and event B are independent events.
The probability that event A will happen is 0.4

Core skill The probability that event B will happen is 0.7

(a) Complete the probability tree diagram. **(2)**

Event A   Event B

                                           0.7 → will happen
                   0.4 → will happen ⟨
                                           ☐ → will not happen

                                           ☐ → will happen
                   ☐ → will not happen ⟨
                                           ☐ → will not happen

☐ marks

(b) Work out the probability that event A will happen and event B will not happen.
You must show your working. **(1)**

P(A will happen and B will not happen) = ☐ × ☐ = ☐

Answer: ....

☐ marks

3 Freddie has a fair four-sided spinner.
The sides of the spinner are numbered 1, 2, 3, 4

Freddie spins the spinner three times.

My
marks

(a) What is the probability the spinner will land on 3 each time? **(2)**

P(lands on 3 each time) = $\frac{\square}{\square} \times \frac{\square}{\square} \times \frac{\square}{\square}$

Answer: ....

marks

(b) What is the probability the spinner lands on the same number each time? **(1)**

Answer: ....

marks

4 There are 10 socks in a drawer.
6 of the socks are black.

Core skill   4 of the socks are grey.
Marta takes at random two socks from the drawer at the same time.

(a) Complete the probability tree diagram. **(2)**

```
        1st sock              2nd sock
                               □
                                 ➜ black
                   black ◄
           6                   □
          ──                     ➜ grey
          10

                               □
                                 ➜ black
           □     grey ◄
                               □
                                 ➜ grey
```

(b) Work out the probability that Marta takes two socks of the same colour.
You must show your working. **(2)**

P(black and black) = $\frac{\square}{\square} \times \frac{\square}{\square}$

P(grey and grey) = $\frac{\square}{\square} \times \frac{\square}{\square}$

Answer: ....

marks

Make a plan

☑ **Had a go** **0–4 marks**	☑ **Nearly there** **5–8 marks**	☑ **Nailed it!** **9–11 marks**
Make sure you are confident with basic probability and with multiplying fractions before tackling this tricky topic.	Well done! Always read a question carefully to work out whether the probabilities change for the second event.	Congratulations! Check your answers by remembering that probabilities are always numbers between 0 and 1.

MY TOTAL
MARKS

Answers
on page 124

44 Sampling, averages and range

  You need to be able to calculate the mean, median, mode and range of a set of data. You also need to be able to construct and interpret two-way tables.

1 The scores of seven pupils in a spelling test are given below.

    4   4   9   7   5   2   4

Write down

(a) the median score **(1)**

Answer: ....

(b) the mean score **(1)**

Answer: ....

(c) the range of scores. **(1)**

Answer: ....

2 Each of the members of a group of bats are either male or female and adult or juvenile. The two-way table shows this information.

Complete the table. **(2)**

	Adult	Juvenile	Total
Male	81		120
Female	85	38	
Total			

marks

3 Aaron wants to estimate the average number of children in a family.

Core skill He chooses 30 students at random from his school and asks them how many children they have in their family. He records his results in a frequency table.

Number of children	Frequency
1	5
2	9
3	8
4	6
5	2

(a) Write down the modal number of children. **(1)**

Answer: ....

(b) Calculate the mean number of children per family. **(2)**

Answer: ....

(c) Give one reason why Aaron's method might not be an accurate way to estimate the average number of children in a family. **(1)**

....

4 The table shows the masses, in kg, of 50 cats.

Mass (x kg)	Frequency
$3 \leqslant x < 4$	21
$4 \leqslant x < 5$	17
$5 \leqslant x < 6$	7
$6 \leqslant x < 7$	5

Calculate an estimate for the mean mass of the cats. **(3)**

Answer: .... kg

Make a plan

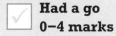 **Had a go**
0–4 marks

Make sure you are confident with knowing how to find each type of average from a list of data. Then you can tackle the core skill of finding averages from tables.

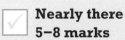 **Nearly there**
5–8 marks

Well done! Use the hints in the answers to work out where you could have picked up more marks. Remember that if a question asks you to calculate the mean of data given in a frequency table, use data value × frequency.

Nailed it!
9–12 marks

Congratulations! Keep an eye out for questions where you have to compare data sets using either the mean, the mode or the median. Always compare the same average for both data sets.

 MY TOTAL MARKS

 Answers on page 125

Revision Guide pages 116, 117, 118

45 Representing data

 You need to be able to interpret and construct tables, charts and diagrams to display different types of data.

1 20 children are asked how many pets they have. The information is recorded below.

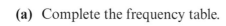

```
2   4   1   0   2
3   1   1   2   3
1   2   2   0   2
2   1   3   2   1
```

(a) Complete the frequency table. **(1)**

Number of pets	Frequency
0	2
1	
2	
3	
4	1

marks

(b) Draw a bar chart to illustrate this information. **(2)**

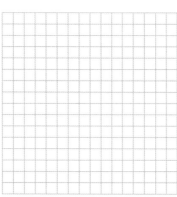

marks

2 The pictogram shows the number of apples Abigail ate each week for a month.

Week 1	🍎 🍎 🍎
Week 2	🍎 🍎
Week 3	🍎 🍎
Week 4	

Key: 🍎 represents 2 apples

(a) How many apples did Abigail eat in week 1? **(1)**

Answer: ....

marks

(b) How many apples did Abigail eat in week 3? **(1)**

Answer: .... marks

Abigail ate 5 apples in week 4.

(c) Use this information to complete the pictogram. **(1)** marks

3 Oladayo draws a bar chart to show the colours of cars that pass the school gates.

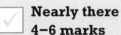

Bar chart: vertical axis labelled "Frequency" from 0 to 18. Horizontal axis labelled "Colour of car" with categories White (17), Silver (14), Black (9), Red (15), Blue (7).

(a) Write down, in simplest form, the ratio of red cars to black cars. **(1)**

Answer: .... marks

Oladayo realises that he has made a mistake.
He has plotted the bar for silver cars correctly, but the ratio of silver cars to blue cars is 7:4

(b) Find the correct height of the bar labelled 'Blue'. **(1)**

Answer: .... marks

Make a plan

✓ **Had a go**
0–3 marks
Make sure you know the names of different types of chart and graph. Revise by looking at an example of each type.

✓ **Nearly there**
4–6 marks
Well done! Use the hints in the answers to work out where you could have picked up more marks. Remember that if a question asks you to draw a graph or chart, you should label the axes – it is nearly always worth a mark in the exam.

✓ **Nailed it!**
7–8 marks
Congratulations! Keep an eye out for questions where you have to describe the similarities and/or differences between two related data sets.

MY TOTAL MARKS

Answers
on page 126

46 Representing data (continued)

 You need to be able to use and interpret scatter graphs, recognise correlation, draw lines of best fit and make predictions based on these. You also need to be able to draw and interpret time series graphs and stem-and-leaf diagrams.

1 The diagram shows a scatter graph.

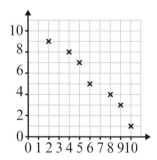

What type of correlation is shown in the scatter graph? **(1)**

Answer: ....

marks

 2 The scatter graph shows the temperature, x°C, and the number of hours of sunshine, y hours.

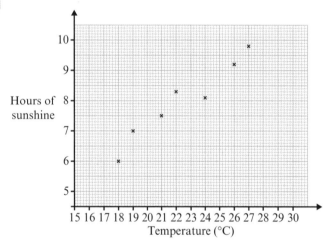

Two more data values are recorded.
There were 8.6 hours of sunshine on a day when the temperature was 24°C and there were 7 hours of sunshine on a day when the temperature was 21°C.

(a) Plot these two points on the scatter graph. **(1)**

marks

(b) Draw a line of best fit on the scatter graph. **(1)**

marks

(c) Describe the type of correlation shown. **(1)**

Answer: ....

marks

(d) Use your line of best fit to estimate the number of hours of sunshine when the temperature is 20°C. **(1)**

Answer: ....

marks

(e) State, with a reason, whether this estimate is likely to be reliable. **(1)**

....

marks

3 The table shows the monthly rainfall in a town over a 6-month period.

Month	April	May	June	July	August	September
Rainfall (mm)	21	15	12	9	10	18

(a) Draw a time series graph to represent this data.　**(2)**

marks

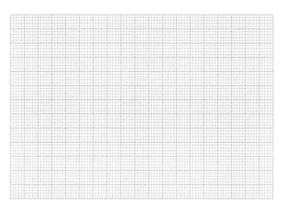

(b) Describe the trend.　**(1)**

marks

....

4 The stem-and-leaf diagram shows the ages of people on a train.

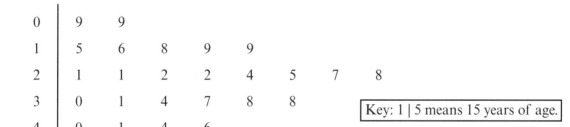

```
0 | 9   9
1 | 5   6   8   9   9
2 | 1   1   2   2   4   5   7   8
3 | 0   1   4   7   8   8
4 | 0   1   4   6
```

Key: 1 | 5 means 15 years of age.

Write down the median age and the range of the ages.　**(2)**

marks

Median: .... years　　　　　　　Range: .... years

---

Answers

Number

1 Whole numbers and decimals

1 $\underline{-6}$ $\underline{-5}$ $\underline{-1}$ $\underline{3}$ $\underline{7}$ $\underline{8}$ ✓

2 $\underline{0.3}$ $\underline{0.315}$ $\underline{0.32}$ $\underline{0.36}$ $\underline{0.374}$ ✓

3 E $\underline{>}$ ✓

4 (a)

(b) $\underline{-4, -3, -2, -1, 0, 1, 2}$ ✓

5 (a) $17 - (-2) = \underline{19}\,°C$ ✓

(b) $-7 - 18 = \underline{-25}\,°C$ ✓

6 (a) $\underline{3000}$ or $\underline{\text{three thousand}}$ ✓

(b) C $\underline{4\,326\,000}$ ✓

7 $14 - 3 \times 5 + 2 = 14 - 15 + 2 = -1 + 2 = 1$

A $\underline{1}$ ✓

8 $(-5 + 11) \div 2$ ✓

$= 6 \div 2 = \underline{3}$ ✓

You may find it useful to draw a number line when attempting to order a list of positive and negative numbers.

The number 0.3 can be written as 0.30. All these numbers have the same number of tenths, 3, so compare the digits in the hundredths column first. The one with the smallest digit is 0.315 so this is the next number.

> means 'is greater than' ⩾ means 'is greater than or equal to'
< means 'is less than' ⩽ means 'is less than or equal to'
= means 'is equal to' ≠ means 'is not equal to'

Use a closed circle ● when the number is included in the interval, that is, for ⩽ or ⩾
Use an open circle ○ when the number is not included in the interval, that is, for < or >

Whole numbers are called integers. If $k < 3$ then 3 is not included. Remember to include 0

Marking
You can use words or figures.

Core skill
You need to be able to apply the BIDMAS rule for the order of operations:
Brackets / **I**ndices / **D**ivision / **M**ultiplication / **A**ddition / **S**ubtraction
The operations must be carried out in the correct order. When you have either multiplication and division, or addition and subtraction, you do the operations in order from left to right. Here you need to do the multiplication first ($3 \times 5 = 15$), followed by the subtraction ($14 - 15 = -1$), then the addition ($-1 + 2 = 1$).

Marking
Score 1 mark for adding the two numbers, and the second mark for dividing by 2

The number halfway between two given values is the mean of the two values. To find the mean of two values, you add them together and divide by 2. You can check your answer using a number line.

2 Factors, multiples, primes and counting

1 **(a)** 2 or 5 or 19 ✔

A prime number has exactly two factors, itself and 1. 1 is not a prime number because it has only 1 factor (itself). 2 is the only even prime number.

(b) 21 ✔

(c) 2 or 6 or 9 ✔

The multiples of a number are all the numbers in its times table.

2

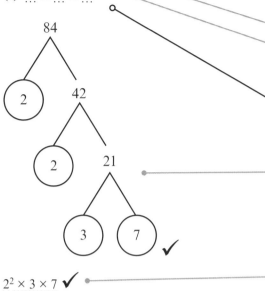

The factors of a number are any whole numbers that divide into it exactly.

Complete the factor tree by using factor pairs of each number, circling the prime factors as you go along. Continue until every branch ends with a prime number. Write down all the circled numbers putting in multiplication signs, and express repeated multiples as powers: $2 \times 2 = 2^2$

$2^2 \times 3 \times 7$ ✔

The numbers in the answer can be written in any order.

3 As a product of its prime factors
$180 = 2^2 \times 3^2 \times 5$ ✔

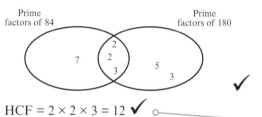

Know the difference between the highest common factor (HCF) and the lowest common multiple (LCM). For any two numbers, the HCF is the largest number that is a factor of both numbers.
You can use a Venn diagram to find the HCF. Write the numbers as a product of their prime factors and put the common factors in the intersection. Then HCF = product of all the prime factors in the intersection.

HCF = $2 \times 2 \times 3 = 12$ ✔

4 Using the Venn diagram completed in Question 3:

The LCM of two numbers is the smallest number that is a multiple of both numbers. In a Venn diagram, the LCM = product of **all** the prime factors.

LCM = $2 \times 2 \times 3 \times 7 \times 3 \times 5 = 1260$ ✔

5 Aces ①   Cobras ②   Diamonds ③

Hot Shots ④   Magpies ⑤   Thunderbolts ⑥

1 vs 2, 1 vs 3, 1 vs 4, 1 vs 5, 1 vs 6

2 vs 3, 2 vs 4, 2 vs 5, 2 vs 6

3 vs 4, 3 vs 5, 3 vs 6

4 vs 5, 4 vs 6

Start by numbering the teams 1 to 6. Each team must play each other team once only so be careful not to count the matches more than once. Remember that 1 vs 2 is the same as 2 vs 1

5 vs 6 ✔

Total of 15 matches ✔

3 Written calculations

1 **(a)**

$47 = 40 + 7$

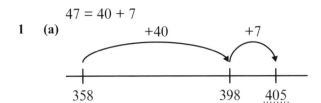

$358 + 47 = \underline{405}$ ✓

> Start from 358 on the number line. Add the tens first then the units.

(b)

$4 + 40 + 85 = 129$

So $185 - 56 = \underline{129}$ ✓

> Start from 56 on the number line. Count on in steps from 56 to 185, then add up the steps to work out the difference between the two numbers.

2 **(a)** $436 \times 24 = 10\,464$

So $4.36 \times 24 = \underline{104.64}$ ✓

> **Core skill**
>
> One of the two numbers that are multiplied together has been divided by 100, so the answer will be divided by 100. Use estimation to check whether you have placed the decimal point correctly. $4.36 \approx 4$, and $24 \approx 20$; $4 \times 20 = 80$, so your answer is correct.

(b) $436 \times 24 = 10\,464$ so $10\,464 \div 24 = 436$

$10\,464 \div 2.4 = \underline{4360}$ ✓

> **Core skill**
>
> Comparing with $10\,464 \div 24 = 436$, the divisor (2.4) is a smaller number so the answer will be greater than 436. 2.4 is one tenth of 24, so the new answer will be 10 times bigger than 436. Checking by estimation: $10\,464 \approx 10\,000$, and $2.4 \approx 2$; $10\,000 \div 2 = 5000$, so your answer is correct.

3 **(a)**

$$\begin{array}{r} 76 \\ \times\ _4 8 \\ \hline 608 \end{array}$$ ✓

So $7.6 \times 0.08 = \underline{0.608}$ ✓

> Ignore the decimal points and multiply the numbers. Count the number of digits on the right-hand side of the numbers in the question (there are 3). There must be the same number of digits on the right-hand side of the decimal point in the answer. Write a 0 before the decimal point.

(b) $\dfrac{8}{\boxed{100}}$ ✓

> **Marking**
>
> Give yourself 1 mark for the digits 608 and the second mark if the decimal point is in the correct position.

4 $\dfrac{44.8}{1.6} = \dfrac{\boxed{448}}{16}$ ✓

$$\begin{array}{r} \boxed{28} \\ 16\overline{)448} \\ -320 \\ 128 \\ -128 \\ \hline 0 \end{array}$$

So $\dfrac{44.8}{1.6} = \underline{28}$ ✓

> Multiply **both** numbers by 10, 100 or 1000 so the second number is a whole number. By creating an equivalent fraction, the final answer will be the same. Work out using long division.

> **Marking**
>
> Give yourself 1 mark for $\dfrac{448}{16}$ and the second mark for the correct answer.

5 Method 1

$$\begin{array}{r} 4\ 6\ 1 \\ \times\ 5\ 8 \\ \hline 3\ 6\ 8\ 8 \\ 2\ 3\ 0\ 5\ 0 \\ \hline 2\ 6\ 7\ 3\ 8 \end{array}$$ ✓✓✓

> This method is sometimes called the column method for multiplication.
> 1 Work out 8×461. (Answer 3688)
> 2 Work out 50×461. Write down 0 then work out 5×461. (Answer 23 050)
> 3 Add the answers. ($3688 + 23\,050 = 26\,738$)

Method 2

This is sometimes called the grid or lattice method.

The answer in this box is the result of multiplying 1 by 5, written with 2 digits as 0 5

Answer: 26 738 ✓

Add the numbers between each set of parallel lines from right to left, carrying into the next set if necessary.

4 Fractions

1 C $\frac{4}{6}$ ✓

Fractions are equivalent if **both** the numerator and the denominator are multiplied (or divided) by the same number.

2 D $\frac{8}{12} + \frac{3}{12}$

$\frac{11}{12}$ ✓

Write both fractions as equivalent fractions with a denominator of 12 before they can be added.

3 C $\frac{3 \times 120}{5} = \frac{360}{5}$

72 ✓

To find a fraction of a number, you multiply the number by the fraction: multiply by the numerator and divide by the denominator.

4 $\frac{12}{1} \div \frac{3}{4} = \frac{12}{1} \times \frac{4}{3}$ ✓

$= \frac{48}{3}$

$= 16$ ✓

> **Core skill**
>
> Show all your working when dividing by a fraction. If the first number is a whole number, you may find it easier to write it as a fraction, for example, $\frac{12}{1} \div \frac{3}{4}$. Then turn the second fraction 'upside down' and change the division to a multiplication. Multiply the numerators together and multiply the denominators together.

5 $2\frac{3}{5} = \frac{\boxed{13}}{5}$ $3\frac{1}{2} = \frac{\boxed{7}}{2}$

$2\frac{3}{5} + 3\frac{1}{2} = \frac{26 + 35}{10}$ ✓

$= 6\frac{1}{10}$ or $\frac{61}{10}$ ✓

> **Marking**
>
> Give yourself 1 mark for writing $12 \times \frac{4}{3}$ or $\frac{12}{1} \times \frac{4}{3}$ and 1 mark for the correct answer.

> **Core skill**
>
> Always convert mixed numbers to improper fractions first, then find a common denominator in order to add. Read the question carefully to see if your answer must be in a specific form.

6 $2\frac{1}{3} \times 3\frac{3}{4} = \frac{7}{3} \times \frac{15}{4}$ ✓

$= \frac{35}{4} = 8\frac{3}{4}$ ✓

> **Marking**
>
> Give yourself 1 mark if you got at least two of the three boxes/lines in the working correct and the second mark for a correct final answer.

Convert both mixed numbers to improper fractions and multiply numerators and multiply denominators. If you cancel the 3 with the 15 at the first stage, you will multiply smaller numbers.

7 $3\frac{1}{2} \div \frac{1}{3}$ ✓

$= \frac{7}{2} \div \frac{1}{3} = \frac{7}{2} \times \frac{3}{1} = \frac{21}{2}$ or $10\frac{1}{2}$ ✓

Number of full glasses = 10 ✓

> **Marking**
>
> 1 mark for converting to improper fractions and 1 mark for the correct final answer in the specified format.

This 'sharing problem' requires division. It is a practical problem so you need to round the answer down to find the number of glasses that can be completely filled.

> **Marking**
>
> Give yourself 1 mark for writing the calculation $3\frac{1}{2} \div \frac{1}{3}$ and 1 mark for $\frac{7}{2} \times \frac{3}{1} = \frac{21}{2}$. Score the third mark for interpreting that an answer of $\frac{21}{2} = 10\frac{1}{2}$ means only 10 glasses can be completely filled.

5 Powers and roots

1 **(a)** $\sqrt{121} = \underline{11}$ ✓

> The symbol $\sqrt{}$ means 'square root'. Square roots are the opposite of squares.

(b) $\sqrt[3]{64} = \underline{4}$ ✓

> The symbol $\sqrt[3]{}$ means 'cube root'. Cube roots are the opposite of cubes.

2 **(a)** $5^0 = \underline{1}$ ✓

> Use $a^0 = 1$

(b) $5^{-2} = \frac{1}{5^2} = \underline{\frac{1}{25}}$ ✓

> Use $a^{-n} = \frac{1}{a^n}$

(c) $100 - (-4)^3 = 100 - (-4 \times -4 \times -4)$
$\qquad\qquad\qquad = 100 - (-64) = 100 + 64 = \underline{164}$ ✓

> You need to follow the BIDMAS rule and work out the indices first.
> Any odd power of a negative number gives a negative answer. Remember that subtracting a negative number makes it positive.

3 **(a)** $3^5 \times 3^3 = 3^{5+3} = \underline{3^8}$ ✓

(b) $(3^2)^3 = 3^{2 \times 3} = \underline{3^6}$ ✓

(c) $\frac{3^4 \times 3^2}{3} = \frac{3^{4+2}}{3^1} = 3^{6-1} = \underline{3^5}$ ✓

> **Core skill**
> You need to know the laws of indices.
> **(a)** $a^m \times a^n = a^{m+n}$
> **(b)** $(a^m)^n = a^{mn}$
> **(c)** $a^m \div a^n = a^{m-n}$
> You should also remember that $a = a^1$

4 $\left(\frac{2}{5}\right)^{-3} = \left(\boxed{\frac{5}{2}}\right)^3$ ✓

$\qquad = \underline{\frac{125}{8}}$ ✓

> Use $\left(\frac{a}{b}\right)^{-n} = \left(\frac{b}{a}\right)^n$ to write $\left(\frac{2}{5}\right)^{-3} = \left(\frac{5}{2}\right)^3$ then cube the numerator and denominator.

5 $(\sqrt{3})^4 = \underline{\sqrt{3}} \times \underline{\sqrt{3}} \times \underline{\sqrt{3}} \times \underline{\sqrt{3}}$ ✓

$(\sqrt{3})^4 = 3 \times 3 = \underline{9}$ ✓

6 Standard form

> Use $\sqrt{a} \times \sqrt{a} = a$

1 $65\,000 = \underline{6.5 \times 10^4}$ ✓

> You can count decimal places to convert between ordinary numbers and standard form. $65\,000 > 10$ so the power of 10 is positive.

2 $5.2 \times 10^5 = \underline{520\,000}$ ✓

3 $0.000\,43 = \underline{4.3 \times 10^{-4}}$ ✓

> $0.000\,43 < 1$ so the power of 10 is negative.

4 $2.6 \times 10^3 = 2600 \quad 2.6 \quad 260 \quad 2.6 \times 10^{-5} = 0.000026$
$\qquad\quad ④ \qquad\qquad ② \quad ③ \qquad\qquad ①$

> First write each number as an ordinary number so you can compare them.

$\underline{2.6 \times 10^{-5}} \quad \underline{2.6} \quad \underline{260} \quad \underline{2.6 \times 10^3}$ ✓

> **Marking**
> 1 mark for correctly converting both numbers to ordinary numbers and 1 mark for the correct final answer.

5 $6.7 \times 10^6 = \underline{6\,700\,000} \qquad 6\,700\,000$
$3.4 \times 10^5 = \underline{340\,000}$ ✓ $\quad + 340\,000$
$\qquad\qquad\qquad\qquad\overline{7\,040\,000} = \underline{7.04 \times 10^6}$ ✓

> **Core skill**
> When adding and subtracting numbers in standard form without a calculator, make sure you write them as ordinary numbers for the calculation and line them up by place value. Write your answer in standard form if necessary.

6 $(4.3 \times 10^7) \times (5 \times 10^{-1}) = (4.3 \times 5) \times (\underline{10^7 \times 10^{-1}})$ ✓

$\qquad = 21.5 \times 10^{(7-1)}$

$\qquad = 21.5 \times 10^6 = \underline{2.15 \times 10^7}$ ✓

> **Core skill**
> When multiplying and dividing numbers in standard form without a calculator, rearrange so that the powers of 10 are together. Multiply or divide the number parts and apply the rules of indices to the powers of 10.
> Rewrite your answer in standard form if necessary.

7 $(1.4 \times 10^{-5}) \div (2 \times 10^{-2}) = (1.4 \div 2) \times (\underline{10^{-5} \div 10^{-2}})$ ✓

$\qquad = 0.7 \times 10^{(-5 - (-2))}$

$\qquad = 0.7 \times 10^{-3} = \underline{7 \times 10^{-4}}$ ✓

> Divide the number parts then subtract the powers of 10. Make sure you write your final answer in standard form.

8 $(1.5 \times 10^8) \div (4 \times 10^5) = (1.5 \div 4) \times (10^8 \div 10^5)$ ✓

$\qquad = 0.375 \times 10^{(8-5)}$

> Divide the larger number by the smaller number to work out how many times bigger it is.

$\qquad = 0.375 \times 10^3 = \underline{375}$ times further ✓

7 Calculator skills

1 $6.25^2 = \underline{39.0625}$ ✓

You can use the $\boxed{x^2}$ key to square a number.

2 $\sqrt{15.21} = \underline{3.9}$ ✓

You can use the $\boxed{\sqrt{\Box}}$ key to work out the square root of a number.

3   **(a)** $\dfrac{1}{3.2} = \underline{0.3125}$ ✓

       (b) $\dfrac{1}{6.4 \times 10^{-3}} = \underline{156.25}$ ✓

The reciprocal of a is $\frac{1}{a}$; it can also be written as a^{-1}. You can find the reciprocal of a number on your calculator by using the $\boxed{x^{-1}}$ key.

You can enter numbers in standard form using the $\boxed{\times 10^x}$ key. You should use the $\boxed{(-)}$ key to enter a negative number.

4 $(3.6 - 0.55)^2 = \underline{9.3025}$

      $\sqrt[3]{10.648} = \underline{2.2}$ ✓

      $9.3025 + 2.2 = \underline{11.5025}$ ✓

Marking

Give yourself 1 mark for correctly completing at least one of the first two answers, then another mark for the correct final answer.

Work out the two terms separately and write them both down before adding.
You can use the $\boxed{\sqrt{\Box}}$ key to find the cube root of a number. You may need to press the shift key first.
You may need to use the $\boxed{S \lozenge D}$ key to change your answer from a fraction or surd to a decimal. Not all calculators have this key.
You can also use the $\boxed{Ans}$ key to use your previous answer in a calculation.

5 $\sqrt{12.5 + 3.4} = \underline{3.987480407}$

      $4.2^3 = \underline{74.088}$ ✓

      $3.987480407 \div 74.088$

      $= \underline{0.053820867(18...)}$ ✓

Marking

Give yourself 1 mark for correctly completing at least one of the first two answers.

Work out the numerator (top) and denominator (bottom) separately and write them both down before dividing.
You can use the $\boxed{x^3}$ key to cube a number.
You are asked to write down all the figures on your calculator display so do not round your answer.

6 $(3.72 \times 10^{-4}) \times (2.1 \times 10^7) = 7812$

                        $= \underline{7.812 \times 10^3}$ ✓ ✓

Marking

Give yourself 1 mark for the correct answer provided you have all the digits up to the bracket.

Marking

Give yourself 1 mark for each part of the final answer (7.812 and 10^3)

7 $\dfrac{2.625 \times 10^5}{5.25 \times 10^{-3}} = (2.625 \times 10^5) \div (5.25 \times 10^{-3})$

               $= 50\,000\,000 = \underline{5 \times 10^7}$ ✓ ✓

Core skill

When working with numbers in standard form using a calculator, it is a good idea to put brackets around each number. Remember, for the answer to be in standard form $A \times 10^n$, then $1 \leqslant A < 10$ and n is an integer.

Marking

Give yourself 1 mark for each part of the final answer (5 and 10^7)

Core skill

You could use the fraction key $\boxed{\blacksquare}$ to work out this calculation. You need to check you have entered the numbers correctly when you do the whole calculation on your calculator, or you could end up with no marks for the question. It is very important that you are familiar with your own calculator so you can use it efficiently.

8 Rounding and estimation

1 $56.4917 = \underline{56.49}$ to 2 d.p. ✔

> To round a number to a given number of decimal places, look at the next digit to the right on a place value diagram. If it is 5 or more, round up; if less than 5, round down.

2   **(a)** $13\,541\,\text{g} = \underline{13\,500}\,\text{g}$ to 3 s.f. ✔

(b) $0.001\,256\,3\,\text{kg} = \underline{0.001\,26}\,\text{kg}$ to 3 s.f. ✔

> Start counting significant figures from the first non-zero digit on the left. Keep place value the same by using zeros as placeholders in whole numbers.

3 $5.23 \approx \underline{5}$

$3.47 \approx \underline{3}$

$0.472 \approx \underline{0.5}$ ✔

> The first three zeros are not significant. For numbers less than 1, do not add any zeros after you have written the correct number of significant figures.

So $\dfrac{5.23 \times 3.47}{0.472} \approx \dfrac{5 \times 3}{0.5} = \dfrac{15}{0.5} = \dfrac{30}{1} = \underline{30}$ ✔

(×2 applied to top and bottom)

> **Core skill**
> For estimation questions, round each number in the calculation to 1 significant figure.
> The symbol $\approx$ means 'approximately equal to'.
> On a non-calculator paper, if the fraction involves a decimal in the denominator you need to eliminate it by multiplying both the numerator and denominator by 10. If the number in the denominator ends with 5 after the decimal point, as in this question, you can multiply the numerator and denominator by 2

4 $\underline{92.5}\,\text{cm}$ ✔

> In this type of question, it helps to draw a number line to work out the greatest and least possible values.
> Counting in 5s:
>
>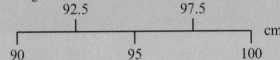
>
> The length is closer to 95 cm than 90 cm or 100 cm, so must lie between the halfway points, 92.5 and 97.5 cm.

5   maximum capacity $= \underline{160.5}\,\text{ml}$

minimum capacity $= \underline{159.5}\,\text{ml}$ ✔

Error interval is $\underline{159.5 \leqslant C < 160.5}$ ✔

> **Core skill**
> Use inequalities to show the error interval when a number is rounded.
> As $C = 160\,\text{ml}$ to the nearest ml, $159.5 \leqslant C < 160.5$, where 159.5 is the minimum capacity and 160.5 is the maximum capacity. $\leqslant$ means 'is less than or equal to' and $<$ means 'is less than'.
> Notice that the maximum capacity is not included in the error interval. If the capacity was 160.5, it would be rounded (up) to 161 ml.

6   **(a)** $£9.95 \approx £10$

$28 \approx 30$

Estimate for ticket sales $= 10 \times 30 = \underline{£300}$ ✔

(b) Estimate for amount paid to charity $= 300 - 160$
$\qquad\qquad\qquad\qquad = \underline{£140}$ ✔

(c) Can overestimate because my answer to part (a) is an overestimate ✔

> In part (a), round each value to 1 significant figure and multiply to find the total cost.
> In part (b) subtract £160 from the estimate in part (a). Both figures in part (a) are rounded up, so your answer for the total amount from the sale of the tickets is an overestimate. Therefore the answer to part (b) is also an overestimate.

7 Least possible value = 5.3

Greatest value is 5.4 ✔

Error interval is $5.3 \leqslant n < 5.4$ ✔

Marking

Give yourself 1 mark for identifying 5.3 or 5.4

This is an example of a truncated number. This is when you look only at the first few digits and ignore all the rest without rounding. In this example, only the first two digits are given, and because you don't know the value of the digit after the 3, all you can say is that the number is at least as big as 5.3 so this is the least possible value of the number. The next digit could be anything up to 9, so the greatest possible value is anything up to but not including 5.4

Algebra

9 Algebraic expressions

1 $2x$ ✔

There are two xs added together.

2 **B** x^3 ✔

Multiplying the same letter together three times gives the power (index) 3

3 **C** ab ✔

In algebra, you don't write the multiplication sign between letters or between numbers and letters.

4 $6x$ ✔

Marking

No marks for writing $6 \times x$

5 $7x + y$ or $y + 7x$ ✔

Core skill

Collect like terms – add together the x terms and the y terms. Take care with the signs of the terms.

6 x^{11} ✔

7 x^{10} ✔

The order of the terms does not matter.

8 $4 \times 3 = 12$ ✔

Add the indices, using $a^m \times a^n = a^{m+n}$

9 $3 \times 6 - 1 = 18 - 1 = 17$ ✔

Multiply the indices, using $(a^m)^n = a^{mn}$

10 $3^2 - 1 = 9 - 1 = 8$ ✔

11 $2 \times -1 + 5 = -2 + 5 = 3$

Core skill

Replace the letter with the given value. You can use a calculator to check your answer.

D 3 ✔

Substitute $x = 3$ and square it before subtracting 1.

12 $2 + 5 \times -4 = 2 + -20 = -18$ ✔

Do the multiplication first. Take care with negative numbers.

13 $2 \times 7 + 5 \times -1 - 3 \times 2 = 14 - 5 - 6 = 3$ ✔

Substitute the given values, and do the multiplications before the additions/subtractions.

10 Formulae

1 **(a)** $3 \times 7 = 21$

$F = 21$ ✔

Divide both sides by a

(b) $\frac{F}{a} = \frac{ma}{a}$

Use BIDMAS.

$m = \frac{F}{a}$ ✔

Subtract at from both sides.

2 **(a)** $v = 4 + 2 \times 3 = 4 + 6 = 10$ ✔

Core skill

To write a formula, use the letters and any values given in the question. Check that your units are consistent.

(b) $u = v - at$ ✔

3 **(a)** $C = 3 + 0.5m$ ✔

C is given in pounds, so you must convert the 50 pence per mile into pounds.

(b) $3 + 0.5 \times 7 = 3 + 3.5 = 6.5$

£6.50 ✔

Substitute 7 for m into your formula in part (a).

(c) $18.5 = 3 + 0.5m$

$15.5 = 0.5m$

$m = \underline{31}$ miles ✔

> Work backwards from your formula in part (a).

> Remember to include the '$T =$' to create a formula.

> Use your formula from part (a) and remember to give your answer in £.

4 (a) $T = \underline{12x + 25y}$ ✔

(b) $T = 12 \times 8 + 25 \times 6$

$= 96 + 150 = 246$ pence

$= \underline{£2.46}$ ✔

5 $\dfrac{E}{m} = c^2$ ✔

$c = \sqrt{\dfrac{E}{m}}$ ✔

Core skill

1 mark for dividing by m and 1 mark for the correct final answer.

> Use inverse operations. In the incorrect answer, the c term should be positive.

6 D $b = \dfrac{A - c}{2}$ ✔

11 Brackets and factorising

1 $3(2a - 5) = 3 \times 2a + 3 \times -5$

$= \underline{6a - 15}$ ✔

> Multiply each term inside the bracket by the term outside.

> $a \times a = a^2$

2 $\underline{3a - a^2}$ ✔

> 8 and 6 share a common factor of 2

3 $8x + 6y = \underline{2(4x + 3y)}$ ✔

> $4x^2$ and $6x$ share a highest common factor of $2x$. Put this term outside the bracket.

4 $4x^2 - 6x = \underline{2x(2x - 3)}$ ✔✔

Marking

Score 2 marks for a complete correct factorisation.
A partial factorisation such as $x(4x - 6)$ or $2(2x^2 - 3x)$ scores only 1 mark.

5 $(x + 4)(x - 3) = x^2 - 3x + 4x - 12$

$= \underline{x^2 + x - 12}$ ✔

Core skill

To expand the brackets, remember FOIL: **F**irst terms, **O**uter terms, **I**nner terms, **L**ast terms. Make sure you simplify your answer by gathering all the like terms together.

6 B $\underline{(x - 7)(x + 2)}$ ✔

Core skill

Look for two numbers that multiply together to give the number on the end and add together to give the number in front of the x term.

7 $\underline{(x + 10)(x - 2)}$ or $\underline{(x - 2)(x + 10)}$ ✔

> $-14 = -7 \times 2$ and $-5 = -7 + 2$

> The brackets can be in either order.

8 $3(x + 7) + 5(2x - 3) = \underline{3x + 21 + 10x - 15}$ ✔

$= \underline{13x} + \underline{6}$ ✔

9 B $\underline{(a - b)(a + b)}$ ✔

> $a^2 - b^2$ is the difference of two squares. You should learn the equivalent form.

> $64 = 8^2$ so this is a difference of two squares.

10 $\underline{(x - 8)(x + 8)}$ or $\underline{(x + 8)(x - 8)}$ ✔

12 Definitions and proof

An expression does not include an = sign.

1 $3(x + 2)$ is an example of an expression. ✔

An equation is true only for some values of the variable. In this case, $x = 3$

2   **D** $3x - 1 = 8$ ✔

A term is a single building block of algebra.

3   **A** $7y$ is a term ✔

4 $x > 3$ is an example of an inequality. ✔

Look for the use of $<$, $\leqslant$, $>$ and $\geqslant$ symbols to identify inequalities.

5   **A** $2n + 3$ ✔

The next odd number is 2 more than $2n + 1$ so $2n + 1 + 2 = 2n + 3$

6 $(x + y)^2 = (x + y)(x + y)$ ✔

$\qquad\qquad = x^2 + 2xy + y^2$ ✔

Core skill

Write the same bracket down twice and use FOIL to expand the brackets.

7 $2n + (2n + 2) + (2n + 4) = 6n + 6$ ✔

$\qquad\qquad\qquad = 6(n + 1)$ ✔

Marking

Score 1 mark for each correct gap filled in. You do not need brackets around the $2n + 2$ in the first line.

The expression in brackets must be a whole number / an integer. ✔

13 Graphs

1 $(-3, 2)$ ✔

The x-coordinate is 'across' and the y-coordinate is 'up' or 'down'.

2

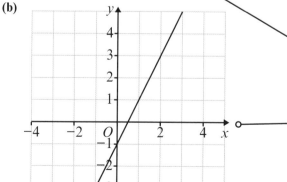

Work out the coordinates of D from the coordinates of A and C.

To find E, work out the coordinates of the midpoint of A and C or B and D.

3   **(a)** $(-3, 4)$ ✔

(b) $(-1, 1)$ ✔ ✔

Marking

In part (b), score 1 mark for each correct coordinate.

Core skill

Substitute the x values into the function to get the corresponding y value. Plot the coordinate points and join them up with a straight line.

4   **(a)** Missing values: $-1, 1, 3$ ✔

(b)

Marking

Score 1 mark only if all three values are correct.

Marking

1 mark for a correctly drawn line joining the points.

5 (a), (b)

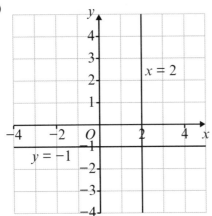

Graphs of the form $x = a$ are vertical lines. Graphs of the form $y = b$ are horizontal lines.

6 (a) Missing values: 3, 2, 1 ✓ ✓ ✓

Marking
Score 1 mark only if all three values are correct.

(b)

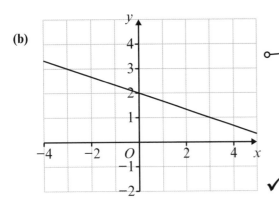

Marking
1 mark for a correctly drawn line joining the points.

✓

14 Straight-line graphs

1 (a) A 5 ✓

When the equation is given in the form $y = mx + c$, the gradient is the number in front of the x.

(b) C (0, −1) ✓

The y-intercept is the coordinate point (0, c).

2 Gradient: 3 ✓

y-intercept: (0, −2) ✓

Core skill

$$\text{Gradient} = \frac{\text{change in } y}{\text{change in } x}$$

3 $y = 4x + 3$ ✓

Use $y = mx + c$ with $m = 4$ and $c = 3$

4 (a) $3 = -2 \times 1 + c$

$3 = -2 + c$

$c = 5$

(0, 5) ✓

Substitute (1, 3) into the equation $y = -2x + c$ to find c.

(b) $y = -2x + 5$ ✓

Marking
If you got part (a) wrong, but used it appropriately in your answer to part (b), you score 1 mark.

5 B $y = 5x + 7$ ✓

6 Gradient: 2

Parallel lines have the same gradient.

y-intercept: (0, 3)

Marking
Score 1 mark for 2x and 1 mark for + 3

$y = 2x + 3$ ✓ ✓

15 Quadratic and curved graphs

1 (a) $(-1)^2 + 3 \times -1 - 2 = 1 - 3 - 2$

$(1)^2 + 3 \times 1 - 2 = 1 + 3 - 2$

Missing values: -4 and 2 ✔ ✔

Core skill

Substitute the x values into the equation to find corresponding y values. Plot the coordinate points and join them up with a smooth curve.

Marking

Score 1 mark for each correct value.

Marking

1 mark for plotting *your* points and 1 mark for plotting all the coordinate points correctly **and** joining them with a smooth curve.

(b)

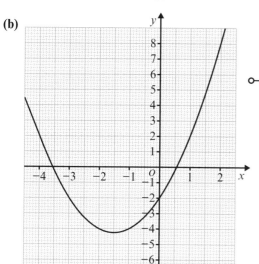

✔ ✔

Make sure you can recognise the basic shapes of positive and negative quadratic and cubic graphs, and reciprocal graphs.

2

✔ ✔

$y = x^3 - x$ $y = x^2 - 2x - 2$ $y = \frac{2}{x}$ $y = 1 + 2x - x^2$

Marking

Score 1 mark for two or three correct and both marks if all four are correct.

Core skill

Read the values from the graph and give them exactly if possible, or rounded to 1 decimal place.

3 (a) $(0, 2)$ ✔

(b) $x = 0.4$ and 4.6 ✔ ✔

Marking

Both values must be correct to 1 decimal place to score the mark.

(c) $(2.5, -4.2)$ ✔

4 (a) $y = x^2 + x - 6 = (x - 2)(x + 3)$

$x = 2$ or -3

A $(2, 0)$ and $(-3, 0)$ ✔

The points where the graph crosses the x-axis are the solutions to the equation $y = 0$

(b) **B** $(0, -6)$ ✔

The value of the y-intercept is the product of the two numbers in the brackets.

16 Real-life graphs

1 (a) £14 ✔

(b) $\frac{17 - 2}{10} = \frac{15}{10}$

1.5 ✔

Read up from 8 on the x-axis and then across to the y-axis.

(c) Cost per mile ✔

The fixed charge is the value of the y-intercept.

(d) £2 ✔

2 (a) 20 km/h ✓

(b) 5 km/h ✓

(c) 25 km ✓

(d) True ✓

Cyclists A and B have both covered the same distance at the point where the graphs cross. Read across to the vertical (distance) axis from this point.

Both cyclists cover the same distance in the same time so they must have the same average speed.

3 **A** The car accelerated during the first 20 seconds. ✓

C The car travelled at a constant speed between 30 and 50 seconds. ✓

Acceleration is shown by an upward sloping line, constant speed by a horizontal line and deceleration by a downward sloping line. The steeper the line, the faster the rate of acceleration or deceleration.

17 Linear equations

1 **C** 15 ✓

2 24 ✓

Add 7 to both sides.

3 $3x - 5 = 1$

$3x = 6$

$x = 6 \div 3 = 2$

Multiply both sides by 4

B $x = 2$ ✓

Add 5 to both sides before dividing by 3

4 $3x - 2 = x + 8$

$2x - 2 = 8$

$2x = 10$

$x = 10 \div 2 = 5$

Start by subtracting x from both sides so that there is only one x term.

C 5 ✓

5 $5x - 6 = 2x + 27$

$3x - 6 = 27$

$3x = 33$ ✓

Start by subtracting $2x$ from both sides so that there is only one x term.

$x = 11$ ✓

Marking

Score 1 mark for getting either $3x$ or 33 and 1 mark for the correct final answer.

6 (a) $12x - 28$ ✓

(b) $4(3x - 7) = 2$

'Hence' usually means use the answer you've just worked out. In this case, the expanded expression in part (a).

$12x - 28 = 2$

$12x = 30$ ✓

Marking

Score 1 mark for $12x = 30$ and 1 mark for the correct final answer.

$x = 2.5$ ✓

First expand the brackets, then use inverse operations. Don't be put off by negative or fractional answers.

7 $7(2x + 5) = -9$

$14x + 35 = -9$

Marking

Score 1 mark for getting either $14x$ or -44, and 1 mark for the correct, simplified final answer.

$14x = -44$ ✓

$x = -\dfrac{22}{7}$ ✓

18 Harder equations

1 **(a)** $(x - 6)(x - 1)$ ✔

(b) $x = 6$ or $x = 1$ ✔

2 $(x - 10)(x - 2) = 0$ ✔

$x = 10$ or $x = 2$ ✔

3 $x = 5$ or $x = -5$ ✔

4 **(a)** $x(x - 7)$ ✔

(b) $x = 0$ or $x = 7$ ✔

5 **D** $x = 1, y = 2$ ✔

6 $2x - 4y = 4$
$+ 6x + 4y = 28$ ✔

$8x = 32$ ✔

$x = 4$

$x = 4, y = 1$ ✔

19 Inequalities and using algebra

1 **(a)** $x < 3$ ✔

(b)

✔

2 $4x - 7 \geqslant 21$

$4x \geqslant 28$

B $x \geqslant 7$ ✔

3 $15 \leqslant 3x < 24$

$5 \leqslant x < 8$

$5, 6, 7$ ✔

4 **(a)** $x + 1 + 2x - 1 + 3x - 2 = 6x - 2$ ✔

(b) $6x - 2 = 19$

$6x = 21$

$x = 3.5$ ✔

5 **(a)** $2x + 4y = 31$ ✔

$4x + 5y = 50$ ✔

(b) **C** Adult: £7.50; Child: £4 ✔

You can substitute each pair of values in both equations rather than solving the equations simultaneously.

20 Sequences

The term-to-term rule is 'add 2'

1 11 ✔

The question asks for the third and fourth terms so don't give the second term.

2 **C** 13 and 16 ✔

Substitute $n = 1$, 2 and 3 into the expression for the nth term.

3 2 5 10 ✔

4 The difference between the terms is 3

The zero term is 2

Hence the nth term = $3n + 2$ ✔✔

5 23 and 37 ✔✔

6 243 ✔

7 **(a)** 48 ✔

(b) 63 ✔

This is a geometric progression. You multiply each term by 3 to get the next term.

8 **C** $13 - 3n$ ✔

Substitute $n = 9$ into the expression for the nth term.

You can try a few values for n.

Ratio and proportion

21 Units and measuring

1 **(a)** $AB = 6.5$ cm ✔

The difference between terms is -3 and the zero term is 13.

(b) 110° ✔

2 2 °C ✔

Remember to start measuring the line at the 0 mark on your ruler

Angle x is obtuse, so your answer should lie between 90° and 180°.

When reading scales, first work out what each division on the scale represents. There are 5 divisions between 0 °C and 5 °C so each division represents 1 °C.

3   4̲8̲0̲ g ✔ •——————————

There are 10 divisions between 400 g and 500 g so each division represents 10 g.

4   3̲4̲ mph ✔ ○

There are 2 divisions between 20 mph and 40 mph so each division represents 10 mph. The reading is just less than halfway between the mark for 30 mph and 40 mph, so 34 mph would be a good estimate.

5   6̲6̲0̲ ml ✔ •

There are 10 divisions between 600 ml and 800 ml so each division represents $200 \div 10 = 20$ ml.

6   **(a)** $3 \times 10 = 3̲0̲$ mm ✔ ○

Core skill

Convert between metric units by multiplying or dividing by 10, 100 or 1000. Think about the relative sizes of the units to sense-check your answer.

   (b) $560 \div 100 = 5̲.̲6̲$ m ✔ •

7   **(a)** $8500 \div 1000 = 8̲.̲5̲$ litres ✔ ○

In (a), a mm is a smaller unit than a cm so the number will be larger. In (b), a metre is a larger unit than a cm so the number will be smaller.

   (b) $7.6 \times 1000 = 7̲6̲0̲0̲$ g ✔ •

$$\overset{\div 10}{\frown} \qquad \overset{\div 100}{\frown}$$

Core skill

Metric units for weight and volume or capacity are connected in the same way as those for length.

8 $23\,000$ mm $= 2300$ cm $= 2̲3̲$ m ✔

In (a), a litre is a larger unit than a ml so the number will be smaller. In (b), a gram is a smaller unit than a kg so the number will be larger.

22 Maps and scale drawings

1   **(a)** 0̲5̲0̲° ✔ •——————

Bearings are measured clockwise from north. They always have 3 figures, so you add zeros if the angle is less than 100°.

   (b) $360 - 120$ ✔

       $= 2̲4̲0̲°$ ✔ ○

Use angles at a point add up to 360° to work out the bearing of *B* from *P*. Point north from *P* and work out the total angle you need to turn through clockwise to point in the direction of *B*.

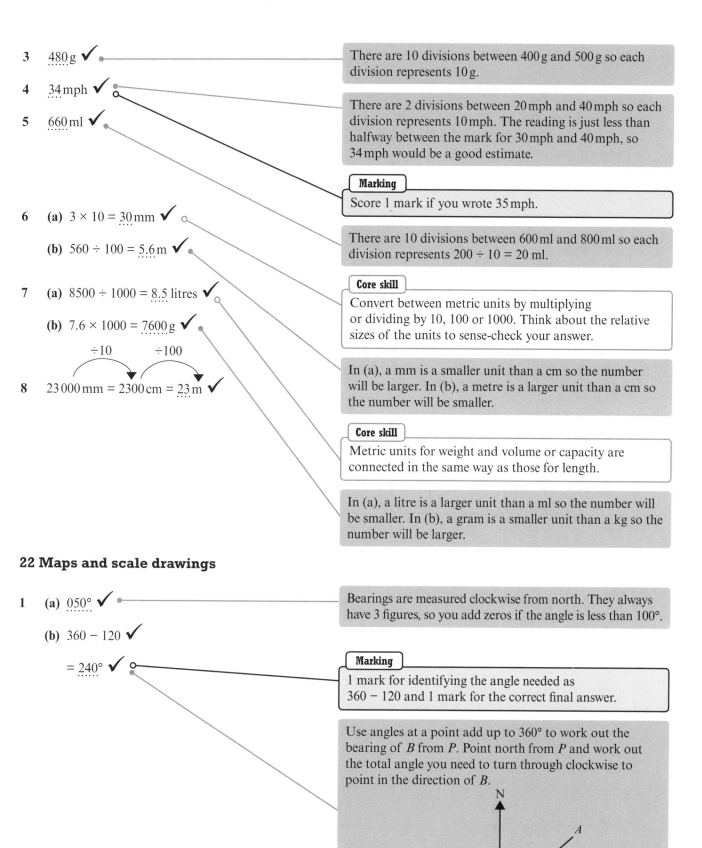

2 $180 + 50 = \underline{230°}$ ✔ ─────

Angles on a straight line add up to 180°.

3 **(a)** $AB = 7\,\text{cm}$ ○─────

> **Core skill**
> The scale means that every 1 cm on the map represents a real distance of 5 km.

Scale is $1\,\text{cm} = 5\,\text{km}$

Real distance $= 7 \times 5 = \underline{35\,\text{km}}$ ✔ ●─

To convert from a distance on the map in cm to the real distance in km, multiply by 5

(b) $\underline{100°}$ ✔

(c) $BC = 30 \div 5 = 6\,\text{cm}$

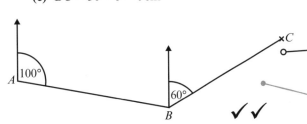

$100°$ $60°$ A B $\times C$ ✔ ✔

> **Marking**
> Give yourself 1 mark for a length of 6 cm and 1 mark for an angle of 60° correctly drawn.

To convert from a real distance in km to a distance on the map in cm, divide by 5

4 $8.5 \times 50\,000 = \underline{425\,000\,\text{cm}}$ ✔ ○─

> **Marking**
> To score 1 mark you need to have completed both parts correctly.

$\overset{\div 100}{\frown}\ \overset{\div 1000}{\frown}$

$425\,000\,\text{cm} = 4250\,\text{m} = \underline{4.25\,\text{km}}$ ✔ ●

Multiplying by 50 000 will give the actual length in cm, so convert to km by first dividing by 100 to find the length in metres, then dividing by 1000 to convert to km.

5 $4.8\,\text{m} = 4.8 \times 100 = 480\,\text{cm}$

$480 \div 32$ ✔

$= \underline{15\,\text{cm}}$ ✔ ●─

Make sure you work with consistent units. You are asked to find the length in cm, so first convert 4.8 m to cm. The actual car is 32 times bigger than the model, so divide by 32

23 Ratio

To write one number as a fraction of another number, write the first as the numerator and the second as the denominator. Then look for any common factors to cancel.

1 **(a)** $\dfrac{320}{840} = \dfrac{32}{84} = \underline{\dfrac{8}{21}}$ ✔ ●─

(b) $320 + 840 = 1160$

You need to express as a fraction of the **total** number of balls so add.

$\dfrac{320}{1160} = \dfrac{32}{116} = \underline{\dfrac{8}{29}}$ ✔ ●

2 C $\underline{27:12}$ ✔ ●─

Equivalent ratios follow the same rules as equivalent fractions – multiply or divide both parts by the same

3 $18:15 = \underline{6:5}$ ✔ ●─

$\overset{\times 3}{\frown}$
$\text{number. } \dfrac{9}{4} = \dfrac{27}{12}$
$\underset{\times 3}{\smile}$

4 $2.4:5.7 = \boxed{24}:\boxed{57}$ ✔ ○─

$57 \div 24 = 2.375$

$\underline{1:2.375}$ ✔

Write the ratio in the order specified in the question, then divide by the highest common factor.

The numbers in a ratio are usually written as whole numbers, but the question specifies the form $1:n$ so a decimal number is correct.

> **Marking**
> Score 1 mark if both boxes are correct. Score 1 mark for a correct final answer in the required form.

5 £75 = $\boxed{5}$ parts   75 ÷ 5 = £15 ✓

   £$\boxed{15}$ = 1 part ✓

   Total amount of money = 9 × £15 ✓

   £135 ✓

6 number of white cards = 56 ÷ 2 = 28 ✓

   number of black cards = 56 ÷ 2 = 28 ✓

   After 7 white cards removed

   number of white cards = 28 − 7 = 21

   number of black cards = 28

   The ratio of white cards to black cards is 21 : 28 ✓

   21 : 28 = 3 : 4 ✓

24 Ratio (continued)

1 1 : 3 ✓

2 milk chocolates = $\boxed{8}$ parts

   white chocolates = $\boxed{7}$ parts ✓

         total = $\boxed{15}$ parts ✓

   15 parts = 60 chocolates

   1 part = 60 ÷ 15 = 4

   number of milk chocolates (8 parts) = 8 × 4 = 32 ✓

3 2.1 m = $\boxed{7}$ parts   2.1 m = 210 cm

   $\boxed{0.3\,\text{m}}$ = 1 part ✓   0.3 m = 30 cm

   Shorter length = 3 × 30 cm = 90 cm or 0.9 m ✓

   Longer length = 210 − 90 = 120 cm or 1.2 m ✓

4 Ratio is 3 : 5   5 − 3 = 2 parts

   £15 = $\boxed{2}$ parts

   $\boxed{£7.50}$ = 1 part ✓

   Total amount of money = 3 + 5 = 8 parts

   8 parts = 8 × £7.50 ✓

   = £60 ✓

5 Ellie gets $\boxed{4}$ parts

Basim gets $\boxed{5}$ parts

Saira gets $\boxed{4}$ parts + $\boxed{£40}$ ✔ o

Total: 13 parts + £40 = £560

13 parts = £560 − £40 = £520 ✔ o

1 part = 520 ÷ 13 = £40

5 parts = 5 × £40 = £200 ✔

You are told the number of parts for Ellie and Basim and given a connection between Saira's share and Ellie's share. Saira's share must be 4 parts + £40

25 Ratio and proportion

1 Fraction that are vanilla = $\dfrac{\boxed{3}}{\boxed{5}}$ ✔ o

$\frac{2}{5} : \frac{3}{5} = 2:3$ ✔

The order of the ratio is important. You are asked for the ratio of chocolate to vanilla, that is $\frac{2}{5} : \frac{3}{5}$.

2 1 pencil = 13.80 ÷ 12 = £1.15 ✔

20 pencils = 20 × 1.15 = £23 ✔

This is an example of direct proportion when both quantities increase at the same rate. First work out the cost of 1 pencil and scale up to 20 pencils.

	pencil	cost	
×20	1	£1.15	×20
	20	£23	

3 1 cm represents 5 ÷ 4 = 1.25 m ✔

1.25 × 10 = 12.5 m ✔

This is another example of direct proportion.

	cm	m	
×10	1	1.25	×10
	10	12.5	

4 (a) 250 g = $\boxed{2}$ parts o

$\boxed{125}$ g = 1 part ✔

3 parts = 3 × 125 = 375 g

Total weight = 250 + 375 = 625 g ✔

(b) $F:B = \boxed{3}:\boxed{2}$

so $\dfrac{F}{B} = \dfrac{\boxed{3}}{\boxed{2}}$ ✔

$F = \frac{3}{2}B$ or $F = 1.5B$ ✔ o

Core skill

Use the information in the question to work out the value of 1 part and use this to find the maximum total weight. Use the given ratio to form an equation with fractions in terms of F and B and rearrange it to get an equation of the form $F = ...$

The total weight is 5 parts of the ratio, so you could also work out 5 × 125.

5

$\div 4 \left(\begin{array}{l} 4y = 5x \\ y = \frac{5}{4}x \end{array} \right) \div 4$

$\div x \left(\begin{array}{l} y = \frac{5}{4}x \\ \frac{y}{x} = \frac{5}{4} \end{array} \right) \div x$ ✔

so $y:x = 5:4$ ✔

Multiply both sides of $\frac{F}{B} = \frac{3}{2}$ by B.

Rearrange the equation to find $\frac{y}{x}$

26 Percentages

1 (a) 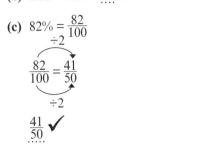 $\frac{1}{5} = \frac{20}{100} = \underset{.....}{20}\%$ ✔

(b) $0.32 \times 100 = \underset{...}{32}\%$ ✔

(c) $82\% = \frac{82}{100}$

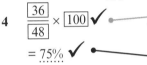 $\frac{82}{100} = \frac{41}{50}$

$\underset{.....}{\frac{41}{50}}$ ✔

To compare a fraction with a decimal, write them in the same form. Writing them as percentages is often the easiest method.

2 $0.7 = \boxed{70}\%$

$\frac{3}{5} = \boxed{60}\%$

$70\% > 60\%$

$\underset{.....}{0.7}$ ✔

25% is equivalent to $\frac{1}{4}$ so an alternative method is
$60 \div 4 = £15$
Learn the common fraction, decimal and percentage equivalents.

3 25% of $£60 = \frac{25}{100} \times 60 = £\underset{...}{15}$ ✔

To write one quantity as a percentage of another:
• divide the first quantity by the second quantity
• multiply your answer by 100

4 $\dfrac{\boxed{36}}{\boxed{48}} \times \boxed{100}$ ✔

$= 75\%$ ✔

Marking
1 mark for all three boxes correct and 1 mark for the correct final answer.

5 Percentage of females $= \boxed{60}\%$

Ratio of males to females $\boxed{40} : \boxed{60}$ ✔

Marking
1 mark for all three boxes correct.

 $40 : 60 = \underset{}{1 : 1.5}$ ✔

When asked to write a ratio in the form $1 : n$, the second part can be a decimal number.

6 $\frac{2}{5} = \boxed{40}\%$

$0.2 = \boxed{20}\%$ ✔

$100 - (28 + 40 + 20)$ ✔

$= 100 - 88 = \underset{..}{12}\%$ ✔

Marking
1 mark for both boxes correct, 1 mark for subtracting the three percentages from 100, and 1 mark for the correct final answer.

27 Proportion

If y is directly proportional to x, the graph of y against x is a straight line, passing through the origin.

If y is directly proportional to x, you can write an equation $y = kx$ where k is a number.

1 C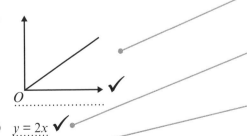

✔

2 D $y = 2x$ ✔

3 (a) $\underset{...}{16}\,\text{km}$ ✔

Read up from 10 miles on the horizontal axis to the graph line, then across to the vertical axis.

(b) $\underset{.........}{\text{kilometres per mile}}$ ✔

4 **C** $y = \frac{10}{x}$ ✔

5 1 kg = $\boxed{1000}$ g

1 g of cashew nuts costs $\dfrac{\boxed{11.79}}{\boxed{1000}}$ ✔

$\dfrac{11.79}{1000} \times 650$ ✔

$= 7.6635$

£7.66 or £7.67 ✔

Marking

Score 1 mark for all three boxes correct, 1 mark for dividing by 1000 and multiplying by 650, and 1 mark for the correct final answer.

Dividing the number of pounds by 1000 gives the price per gram and multiplying by 650 gives the cost of 650 g. Give your answer to 2 decimal places for the correct money format.

6 **(a)** 1 man would take 9×8 days = 72 days ✔

3 men would take $72 \div 3$ ✔

$= 24$ days ✔

Marking

Score 1 mark for writing 9×8, 1 mark for dividing by 3 and 1 mark for the correct final answer.

(b)
$\times 3 \begin{cases} 8 \text{ men} \\ 24 \text{ men} \end{cases}$ $\quad \begin{cases} 9 \text{ days} \\ 3 \text{ days} \end{cases} \div 3$

24 men ✔

This is an inverse proportion problem – fewer men will take a longer time than more men. At each stage of your working, ask yourself whether your answer should be bigger or smaller.

Less time means more men so multiply the number of men by 3

28 Compound measures

1 30 minutes = $\dfrac{\boxed{1}}{\boxed{2}}$ hour

distance = speed × time ✔

$= 125 \times \frac{1}{2} = 62.5$ miles ✔

Learn the number of minutes in common fractions of an hour.

2 density $= \dfrac{\text{mass}}{\text{volume}} = \dfrac{1.5}{0.0008}$ ✔

$= 1875$ kg/m³ ✔

Marking

1 mark for completing the first four parts correctly and 1 mark for the correct final answer.

You need to learn the relationships between density, mass and volume. Remember to state the units with your answer if they are not given.

3 10 m/s = $10 \times 60 \times 60$ m/h = 36000 m/h

$= 36000 \div 1000$ km/h ✔

$= 36$ km/h ✔

Marking

Give yourself 1 mark for either multiplying by 60×60 or for dividing by 1000 and 1 mark for the correct final answer.

If the speed is 10 m/s, it will cover 10×60 metres in 1 minute and $10 \times 60 \times 60$ metres in 1 hour. Divide by 1000 to convert from m/h to km/h.

4 Time = $\boxed{530} \div \boxed{75}$ ✔

$= \boxed{7.0666...}$ minutes

$0.0666 \times 60 = 4$

7 minutes 4 seconds ✔

Marking

1 mark for both boxes correct.

Divide 530 by 75 to find the number of minutes taken to fill the pool. To convert the decimal part of the number to seconds, multiply by 60 because there are 60 seconds in 1 minute.

5 2 hours 15 minutes = $\boxed{2.25}$ or $\boxed{2\frac{1}{4}}$ hours

average speed $= \dfrac{\text{distance}}{\text{time}}$ ✔

$= \dfrac{63}{2.25} = \underline{28}\,\text{km/h}$ ✔

6 $\boxed{25} = \dfrac{\boxed{120}}{A}$

$A = \dfrac{\boxed{120}}{\boxed{25}}$ ✔

$A = \dfrac{120}{25} = \underline{4.8}\ \text{m}^2$ ✔

The formula for pressure is given on the exam paper, but you should try to remember it anyway.
Remember to state the units with your answer if they are not given. In this question, the force is given in newtons and the pressure is given in newtons/m^2 so the area will be in m^2.

29 Percentage change

1 (a) Reduction in price $= \dfrac{\boxed{15}}{\boxed{100}} \times \boxed{60}$ ✔

$= \pounds 9$

Sales price $= 60 - 9 = \pounds\underline{51}$ ✔

(b) D $\underline{44 \div 0.85}$ ✔

The price is reduced, so subtract your answer from the normal price.

2 (a) $100 + 9.5 = 109.5\% = \dfrac{109.5}{100}$

$= \underline{1.095}$ ✔

(b) $100 - 12 = 88\% = \dfrac{88}{100}$

$= \underline{0.88}$ ✔

The normal price is 100% so the sale price is $(100 - 15) = 85\% = 0.85$. To find the normal price, divide the sale price by 0.85

3 Actual increase $= \boxed{132} - \boxed{96}$

Percentage increase $= \dfrac{\text{actual increase}}{\text{original number of sales}} \times 100$ ✔

$= \dfrac{36}{96} \times 100 = \underline{37.5}\%$ ✔

4 Interest for 1 year $= \dfrac{\boxed{2.4}}{\boxed{100}} \times \boxed{600}$ ✔

$= \pounds 14.40$

Interest for 4 years $= 4 \times \boxed{\pounds 14.40}$ ✔

$= \pounds\underline{57.60}$ ✔

To calculate a percentage change:
• work out the amount of change
• write this as a percentage of the original amount.

To work out simple interest:
• work out the amount of interest for 1 year
• multiply your answer by the number of years.
You must give your answer correct to the nearest penny if necessary.

5 **(a)** Multiplier = 1.03 ✓

(b) Total amount = 500 × ⌞1.03⌟^{⌐4⌐} ✓

$500 \times 1.03^4 = 562.754... = £562.75$ ✓

The interest is 3% at the end of the first year so there will be 103% of the original amount in the bank account.

Marking
Both boxes must be correct to score 1 mark.

At end of year 1 the amount of money in the account is 500×1.03. The amount is multiplied by 1.03 every year, so after 4 years, the amount of money in the account is 500×1.03^4

Geometry and measures

30 2-D shapes

1 **(a)** The angle is obtuse ✓

Obtuse angles are greater than 90° but less than 180°.

(b) The triangle is isosceles ✓

An isosceles triangle has a pair of equal angles and a pair of equal sides.

2 Rhombus ✓

3 **(a)** **B** Chord ✓

Core skill
Learn the names and properties of quadrilaterals. Dashes mark edges of equal length and arrows mark parallel edges.

(b) Segment ✓

Chords are lines that join two points on the circumference of a circle.

4 **(a)** (4, 6) ✓

A segment is the piece of a circle cut off by a chord.

(b) (2, 4) ✓

(c) (Right-angled) trapezium ✓

Marking
(2, 0) and (10, 8) are also possible correct answers.

5 **(a)** True ✓

Marking
Give yourself the mark if you wrote 'trapezium'.

(b) False ✓

31 Constructions

Squares have opposite sides equal in length and four right angles.

Not all isosceles triangles have three sides of equal length.

1

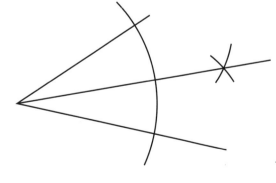

Make sure you show your construction lines.

2

Make sure that you show your construction lines.

115

3

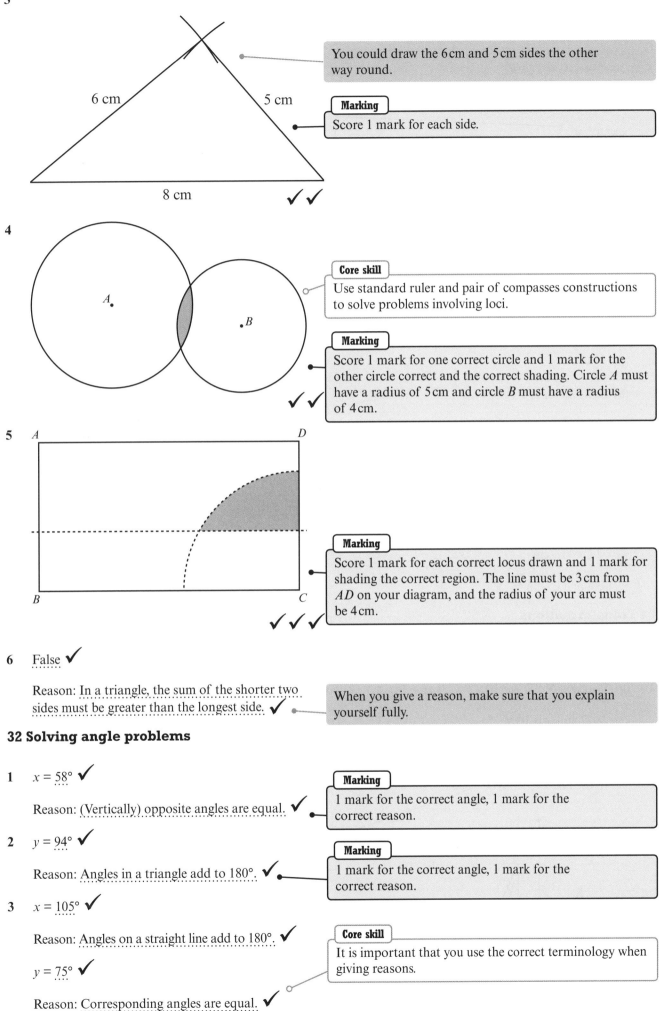

You could draw the 6 cm and 5 cm sides the other way round.

Marking
Score 1 mark for each side.

6 cm   5 cm

8 cm ✓✓

4

Core skill
Use standard ruler and pair of compasses constructions to solve problems involving loci.

Marking
Score 1 mark for one correct circle and 1 mark for the other circle correct and the correct shading. Circle *A* must have a radius of 5 cm and circle *B* must have a radius of 4 cm.

A.   *.B*

✓✓

5   *A*   *D*

Marking
Score 1 mark for each correct locus drawn and 1 mark for shading the correct region. The line must be 3 cm from *AD* on your diagram, and the radius of your arc must be 4 cm.

B   *C*

✓✓✓

6   False ✓

Reason: In a triangle, the sum of the shorter two sides must be greater than the longest side. ✓

When you give a reason, make sure that you explain yourself fully.

32 Solving angle problems

1 $x = 58°$ ✓

Reason: (Vertically) opposite angles are equal. ✓

Marking
1 mark for the correct angle, 1 mark for the correct reason.

2 $y = 94°$ ✓

Reason: Angles in a triangle add to 180°. ✓

Marking
1 mark for the correct angle, 1 mark for the correct reason.

3 $x = 105°$ ✓

Reason: Angles on a straight line add to 180°. ✓

$y = 75°$ ✓

Reason: Corresponding angles are equal. ✓

Core skill
It is important that you use the correct terminology when giving reasons.

4 **(a)** $360 \div 8 = \underline{45}°$ ✓

    (b) $180 - 45 = \underline{135}°$ ✓

5 $2x + 3x + 4x = 180$ ✓

    $9x = 180$

    $x = \underline{20}°$ ✓

33 Similar and congruent shapes

1   **D** SSA ✓

The angle must be **between** the two sides.

2   A and C ✓

Congruent shapes can be rotations of each other but must be the same size.

3   **(a)** $9 : 22.5 = 18 : 45 = \underline{2 : 5}$ ✓

    (b) Scale factor is $\frac{2}{5} = 0.4$

       $37.5 \times 0.4 = \underline{15}\,\text{cm}$ ✓

4   **(a)** $\underline{D}$ ✓

Write the ratio of corresponding sides in the correct order $(XY : AB)$ and simplify.

    (b) Scale factor is $6 \div 8 = 0.75$

       $12 \times 0.75 = \underline{9}\,\text{cm}$ ✓

It might help to draw and carefully label one of the triangles so both triangles are in the same orientation.

5   **A** All squares are similar. ✓

Work out the scale factor, then multiply BC, the side corresponding to EF.

    D All equilateral triangles are similar. ✓

Regular polygons are mathematically similar.

6 $\frac{8}{14} \times 10 = 5.71\,\text{cm}$

    $\frac{8}{10} \times 14 = 11.2\,\text{cm}$

    $\underline{5.71}\,\text{cm or } \underline{11.2}\,\text{cm}$ ✓ ✓

The 8 cm side in rectangle **B** could correspond to either the shorter side or the longer side of rectangle **A**.

The flag moves 3 squares to the right and 2 squares up.

34 Transformations

1 $\underline{\binom{3}{2}}$ ✓ ✓

2   **(a)** Rotation ✓

    $\underline{180° \text{ about } (0, 0)}$ ✓

    (b) Reflection ✓

    $\underline{\text{In the line } x = -1}$ ✓

3

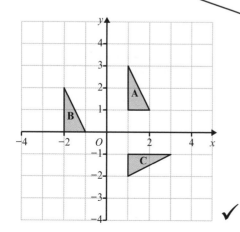

Use tracing paper to help with the rotation.

✓ ✓

4

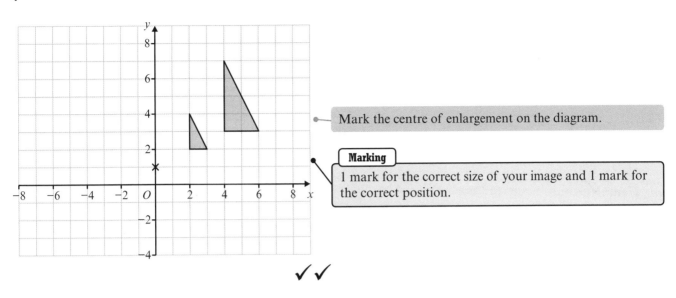

Mark the centre of enlargement on the diagram.

Marking
1 mark for the correct size of your image and 1 mark for the correct position.

✓ ✓

35 Representing 3-D shapes

1 A square-based pyramid has 5 faces, 8 edges and 5 vertices. ✓ ✓ ✓

Visualise the shape to work these out.

Marking
Score 1 mark for each correct number.

2 D Trapezium ✓

A prism has a constant cross-section.

3 (a) Cylinder ✓

(b) Cone ✓

Make sure you use correct mathematical language. You would not score the mark for part (c) if you wrote 'ball'.

(c) Sphere ✓

4 B

Imagine folding the nets up.

Core skill
You need to be able to identify 3-D shapes from plans and elevations.

5 Hexagonal prism ✓

6

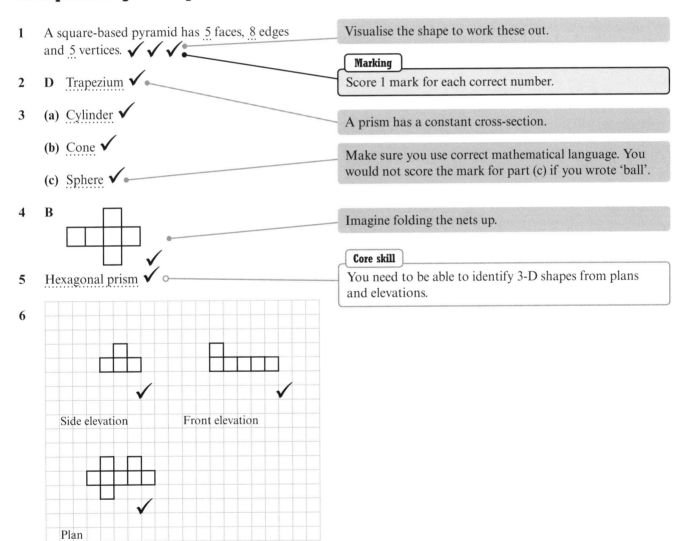

Side elevation ✓   Front elevation ✓

Plan ✓

36 Lengths and areas

> The perimeter is the distance around the edge of the shape.

1 (a) 4×7

    $\underline{28}$ cm ✔

> The area of a square of side length x is x^2.

(b) 7^2

    $\underline{49}$ cm² ✔

2 $\frac{1}{2} \times 9 \times 6$ ○

> **Core skill**
> The formula for the area of a triangle is $A = \frac{1}{2}bh$.

  $\underline{27}$ cm² ✔

> **Core skill**
> The formula for calculating the circumference of a circle is $C = 2\pi r$.
> The formula for calculating the area of a circle is $A = \pi r^2$.

3 (a) $C = 2 \times \pi \times 3 = \underline{18.8}$ cm ✔ ○

(b) $A = \pi \times 3^2 = \underline{28.3}$ cm² ✔

> Unless otherwise stated, you can give your answers to any sensible degree of accuracy, for example 3 s.f. or leave them as exact multiples of π.

4 $A = \pi r^2$

  $81\pi = \pi \times r^2$

  $r = \sqrt{81} = 9$

> Work backwards from the formula for the area of the circle to find r. The question asks you for the diameter, so double the radius.

  Diameter $= 2 \times 9 = \underline{18}$ cm ✔

5 $9 \times 15\,000 = 135\,000$ cm

> First find the value in cm, then divide by 100 to find the distance in m then divide by 1000 to find the distance in km.

  $135\,000$ cm $= 1350$ m $= \underline{1.35}$ km ✔

6 $\underline{211}°$ ✔

> This is called the 'back bearing'. Bearings and back bearings differ by 180°. It might be helpful to draw a sketch map.

7 (a) $\frac{110}{360} \times \pi \times 7^2 = \underline{47.0}$ cm² ✔

(b) $\frac{110}{360} \times 2 \times \pi \times 7$

  Arc length $= 13.4\ldots$ cm

> Add on the two radii to calculate the perimeter of the sector.

  Perimeter $= 13.4 + 7 + 7 = \underline{27.4}$ cm ✔

8 B $\underline{100\,000}$ cm² ✔

> $1\,m^2 = 100 \times 100 = 10\,000\,m^2$, so $10\,m^2 = 100\,000\,m^2$

9 Area of trapezium $= \frac{1}{2}(24 + 17) \times 21 = 430.5$

  Area of parallelogram $= 21 \times 17 = 357$ ✔ ○

> **Marking**
> Score 1 mark for either area correct.

  $430.5 + 357 = \underline{787.5}$ cm² ✔

> Area of a trapezium $= \frac{1}{2}(a + b)h$
> Area of parallelogram $= bh$

37 Volumes and surface areas

1 $4 \times 6 \times 8 = \underline{192}$ cm³ ✔

> The volume of a cuboid with sides l, w and h is lwh.

2 $V = \frac{4}{3}\pi r^3 = \frac{4}{3} \times \pi \times 7^3$

  $= \underline{1440}$ cm³ ✔

> Round your answer to 3 s.f. as instructed.

3 $V = \frac{1}{3}\pi r^2 h = \frac{1}{3} \times \pi \times 6^2 \times 8$

  $= \underline{96\pi}$ cm³ ✔

> Don't convert your answer to a decimal and round because the question asks for an exact multiple of π.

4 $A = 4\pi r^2$

$\quad = 4 \times \pi \times 5^2$

$\quad$ **D** $\underline{100\pi}$ ✔

The formula uses the radius of the sphere and you are given the diameter so halve this first.

5   Area of cross-section: $\frac{5+8}{2} \times 6 = \underline{39}$ cm^2 ✔

Volume: $39 \times 18 = \underline{702}$ cm^3 ✔

> **Core skill**
> Calculate the cross-section area first and then multiply this by the length to find the volume.

> **Marking**
> Score 1 mark for the correct cross-section area and 1 mark for the correct volume.

6 $V = \pi r^2 h$

$\quad h = 180\pi \div (1.5^2 \times \pi)$ ✔

$\quad = \underline{80}$ cm ✔

Divide the volume of the cylinder by the formula for the cross-section area.

> **Marking**
> Score 1 mark for dividing the volume by at least π or 1.5^2
> Score 1 mark is for a complete correct answer.

7 $\frac{30}{18} = \frac{x+5}{x} \Rightarrow \frac{5}{3} = \frac{x+5}{x} \Rightarrow 5x = 3x + 15$ ✔

$\quad x = \underline{7.5}$ ✔

> **Marking**
> Score 1 mark for the correct ratio of side lengths.
> It doesn't have to be written as an equation, or simplified.

38 Right-angled triangles

1 $x^2 = 20^2 + 9^2$

> **Core skill**
> Use Pythagoras' theorem to calculate the missing side length: $c^2 = a^2 + b^2$

$\quad x = \sqrt{481} = \underline{21.9}$ cm ✔

> **Marking**
> Score the mark if you wrote your answer as an exact surd, $\sqrt{481}$

2 $x^2 = 17^2 - 15^2$

$\quad x = \sqrt{64} = \underline{8}$ cm ✔

You are finding a shorter side so $c^2 - a^2 = b^2$.

3 $x = \cos^{-1}\left(\frac{11}{14}\right)$

> **Core skill**
> Remember SOHCAHTOA to help you decide which trigonometric ratio to use.

$\quad x = \underline{38.2}°$ ✔

You are given the adjacent side and the hypotenuse so use cosine.

4 $\tan 25° = \frac{x}{7}$

$\quad x = 7 \times \tan 25°$

$\quad = \underline{3.26}$ cm ✔

You are given the opposite and adjacent sides so use tan.

5   **B** $\underline{\sin 60° \text{ and } \cos 30°}$ ✔

Try putting these values into your calculator.

6   Base angle $= 45°$, shorter side lengths are x ✔

$\quad \tan\theta = \frac{\text{opposite}}{\text{adjacent}}$

$\quad \tan 45° = \frac{x}{x} = 1$ ✔

> **Marking**
> Score 1 mark for writing a base angle and indicating the two shorter sides are x. These can be shown on the diagram. Score 1 mark for relating these to the tan ratio for an angle of 45° and a complete argument.

7   Base of small triangle: $7^2 - 5^2 = 24$ so $\sqrt{24} = \underline{4.89}...$ ✔

Use Pythagoras' theorem to work out the base of the left-hand triangle and trigonometry to work out the base of the right-hand triangle.

$\quad$ Base of large triangle: $\frac{5}{\tan 21°} = 13.03...$ ✔

$\quad x = 4.89... + 13.03... = \underline{17.9}$ cm (3 s.f.) ✔

> **Marking**
> Score 1 mark for using Pythagoras' theorem correctly and 1 mark for using the tan ratio correctly.
> Score the final mark for a complete correct answer, rounded to a sensible degree of accuracy.

39 Vectors

1

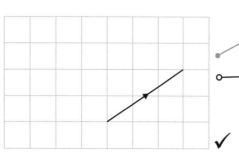

Your answer should include an arrowhead to show the direction of the vector.

Marking

1 mark for drawing the correct vector anywhere on the grid.

✔

2 $\begin{pmatrix} 2 \\ -1 \end{pmatrix}$ ✔

The shape moves 2 spaces to the right and 1 space down.

3 **(a)** $\begin{pmatrix} 4+3 \\ 2-1 \end{pmatrix}$ $\begin{pmatrix} 7 \\ 1 \end{pmatrix}$ ✔

Core skill

To add vectors, add across.
To subtract vectors, subtract across.
To multiply a vector by a scalar, multiply **both** numbers.

(b) $\begin{pmatrix} 3-2 \\ -1+6 \end{pmatrix}$ $\begin{pmatrix} 1 \\ 5 \end{pmatrix}$ ✔

(c) $\begin{pmatrix} 3 \times 3 \\ 3 \times -1 \end{pmatrix}$ $\begin{pmatrix} 9 \\ -3 \end{pmatrix}$ ✔

(d) $\begin{pmatrix} -2-3 \\ 6-(-1) \end{pmatrix}$ $\begin{pmatrix} -5 \\ 7 \end{pmatrix}$ ✔

(e) $\begin{pmatrix} 4 \times 4 \\ 4 \times 2 \end{pmatrix} + \begin{pmatrix} 3 \times 3 \\ 3 \times -1 \end{pmatrix} - \begin{pmatrix} -2 \\ 6 \end{pmatrix}$

$= \begin{pmatrix} 16+9-(-2) \\ 8+(-3)-6 \end{pmatrix}$ $\begin{pmatrix} 27 \\ -1 \end{pmatrix}$ ✔ ✔

Marking

For part (e), score 1 mark for each number.

Solve this problem in the same way as you would solve an equation.

4 $2\mathbf{a} + \begin{pmatrix} 24 \\ -9 \end{pmatrix} = \begin{pmatrix} -8 \\ 20 \end{pmatrix}$ ✔

$2\mathbf{a} = \begin{pmatrix} -32 \\ 29 \end{pmatrix}$ ✔

$\mathbf{a} = \begin{pmatrix} -16 \\ 14.5 \end{pmatrix}$ ✔

Marking

Score 1 mark for substituting and evaluating the 3**b** and 4**c** terms, 1 mark for rearranging to make 2**a** the subject, and 1 mark for a complete correct solution. You can write the *y* vector as a mixed number or as an improper fraction.

Probability and statistics

40 Probability

1 **(a)**

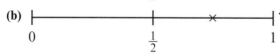

If the spinner is fair, all the outcomes are equally likely. In this question, only 1 out of the 4 possible outcomes is green, so the probability of landing on green is $\frac{1}{4}$

✔

(b)

The probability the spinner will not land on blue is $1 -$ the probability it will land on blue.

$1 - \frac{1}{4} = \frac{3}{4}$

✔

2 **(a)** Total number of pens = 4 + 8 + 12 = 24

Probability (blue pen) = $\frac{8}{24}$ or $\frac{1}{3}$ ✔

Core skill

Probability of an event happening
$= \dfrac{\text{number of successful outcomes}}{\text{total number of possible outcomes}}$
You can write a probability as a fraction, a decimal or a percentage.

(b) R = red, B = blue, G = green

Possible combinations are:

BR   BG   BB   RR   RG   GG ✔ ✔

The combinations are all possible pairings of the pens. RB is the same as BR as the order is not important.

Marking

Score 1 mark for four correct combinations and the second mark for all six correct.

3 (a) P(6) = 1 − (0.14 + 0.08 + 0.16 + 0.12 + 0.19) ✔

       = 0.31 ✔

The probabilities have to add up to 1 as the events are mutually exclusive, which means they cannot happen at the same time. So subtract the sum of the other probabilities from 1

(b) 200 × 0.16 = 32 ✔

Use expected number of outcomes = number of trials × probability

4 (a) Number of boys = 300 − 120 = 180

Number of boys **not** going to
Year 12 = 180 − 155 = 25 ✔ ✔

Number of girls **not** going to
Year 12 = 40 − 25 = 15

Number of girls going to
Year 12 = 120 − 15 = 105

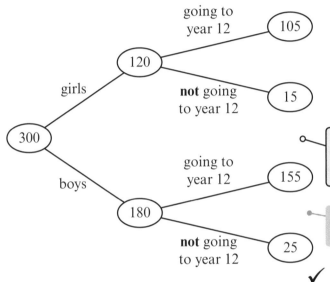

Marking

Score 1 mark if you got at least two of the four values correct, a second mark for all four correct and 1 mark for a correctly completed frequency tree.

In a frequency tree, each frequency is equal to the sum of its branches.

✔

(b) Probability (student is a girl not going on to
Year 12) = $\frac{15}{300}$ or $\frac{1}{20}$ ✔

In probability questions, you do not have to write the answer in its simplest form unless you are specifically asked to.

41 Experimental probability

1 (a)

Score	Tally	Frequency
1–10	I	1
11–20	IIII	4
21–30	JHT	5
31–40	JHT II	7
41–50	IIII	4
51–60	III	3

✔ ✔

Marking

1 mark for 8 out of 12 cells boxes completed correctly and the second mark for all correct.

4 students scored between 41 and 50, 3 students scored between 51 and 60

(b) 4 + 3 = 7 ✔

Add together the frequencies from the first three rows.

(c) 5 + 4 + 1 = 10

    P(score 30 or less) = $\frac{\boxed{10}}{\boxed{24}}$ ✔ ✔

Marking

1 mark for each part of fraction correct. Also accept $\frac{5}{12}$

2 (a)

Set 2 \ Set 1	1	3	5	7	9
2	3	5	7	9	11
4	5	7	9	11	⑬
6	7	9	11	⑬	⑮
8	9	11	⑬	⑮	⑰

Set 1 is the column header across the top; Set 2 is the row header down the side.

A sample space diagram shows all the possible outcomes of two events. There are five numbers in Set 1 and four in Set 2, so the total number of possible outcomes is 5 × 4 = 20

Marking

1 mark for each part of fraction correct. Also accept $\frac{3}{10}$

(b) Number of scores greater than 12 = 6

P(score greater than 12) = $\frac{6}{20}$ ✔ ✔

Core skill

When an experiment is carried out to estimate the probability of something happening, work out the probability of the event using this formula for relative frequency:

$$\text{estimated probability} = \frac{\text{frequency of outcome}}{\text{total frequency}}$$

You can write a probability as a fraction, a decimal or a percentage. You do not need to simplify your fraction.

3 (a) Total number of trials = 20 + 40 + 100 + 60

= 220

Total number of 6s = 3 + 8 + 25 + 12 = 48

Estimated probability = $\frac{48}{220}$ ✔ ✔

Marking

1 mark for two out of four parts correctly completed, 1 mark for all correct.

(b) Theoretical probability = $\frac{1}{6}$ ✔

(c) The friend whose results will give the best estimate for the theoretical probability is Caz because this friend had the highest/largest/greatest number of trials. ✔

Core skill

The theoretical probability is based on the number of times you expect the outcome to happen.

With a fair dice, you would expect to get a 6 once in every six throws.

Probability estimates based on relative frequency are more accurate for a larger number of trials.

42 Venn diagrams

1

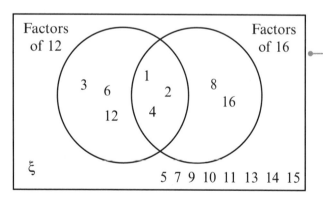

The symbol ξ is used for the universal set. It represents all the elements you have to consider in a question, which in this case is all the integers from 1 to 16. The numbers in the overlap of the two circles are the numbers that are factors of both *A* **and** *B*. When you complete a Venn diagram, make sure you only list each element once.

✔ ✔

The factors of 12 are ①②3④6, 12

The factors of 16 are ①②④8, 16 ✔

Marking

Score 1 mark for working out the factors of 12 or the factors of 16 correctly, 1 mark for correctly completing two of the four sections in the Venn diagram and 1 mark for correctly completing all four sections.

2 (a)

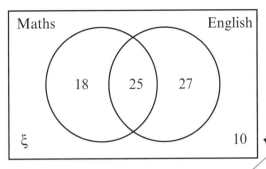

ξ 10 ✔

$52 - 25 = 27$ ✔

$80 - 18 - 25 - 27 = 10$ ✔

Marking

1 mark for working out 27 students study English only, 1 mark for working out 10 students study neither maths nor English, and 1 mark for correct diagram.

P(neither Maths nor English) =

$$\frac{\text{number of students that do not study Maths or English}}{\text{total number of students}}$$

(b) Probability the student studies neither Maths

nor English = $\frac{10}{80}$ or $\frac{1}{8}$ ✔

ξ is all the numbers that appear in the Venn diagram.

Core skill

Learn the different symbols in set notation.
$\cup$ means union: the union of two sets is the set of elements that belong to either set.
$\cap$ means intersection: the intersection of two sets is the set of elements that belong to **both** sets,
A' means not A or A complement: it is everything in ξ that is **not** in A.

3 (a) 11 ✔

(b) (i) $A \cup B = 3, 5, 8, 10, 12, 22, 24$ ✔

(ii) $A \cap B = 3, 5, 8$ ✔

(c) P(number is in set A') = $\boxed{\dfrac{7}{11}}$ ✔ ✔

List the numbers that are in A **or** B.

Count how many numbers are not in A.

Marking

1 mark for each number correct.

43 Combined events

1   **C**   Picking a milk chocolate from a box of milk and dark chocolates, eating it and then picking another milk chocolate. ✔

In a dependent event, the outcome of the second event is affected by the outcome of the first event.

2 (a)

Event A   Event B

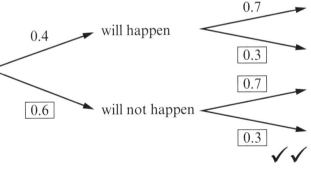

(b) P(A will happen and B will not

happen) = $\boxed{0.4} \times \boxed{0.3} = \boxed{0.12}$ ✔

Core skill

When there are two independent events, the outcome of one does not affect the outcome of the other. You can show independent events on a tree diagram and write the probabilities on the branches. The probabilities on each pair of branches must add up to 1.
For independent events: P(A **and** B) = P(A) × P(B)
For mutually exclusive events: P(A **or** B) = P(A) + P(B)

Marking

Score 1 mark for the correct answer.

3 **(a)** P(lands on 3 each time) $= \boxed{\dfrac{1}{4}} \times \boxed{\dfrac{1}{4}} \times \boxed{\dfrac{1}{4}}$ ✔

$$= \frac{1}{64} \text{ ✔}$$

Score 1 mark for filling in the boxes correctly and 1 mark for the correct answer.

(b) P (lands same number each time) = P (lands on 1 each time) + P (lands on 2 each time) + P (lands on 3 each time) + P (lands on 4 each time)

$$= 4 \times \frac{1}{64} = \frac{1}{16} \text{ ✔}$$

Core skill

You use the same rules for tree diagrams as for independent events when working out the probabilities of combined events.
Be careful when working out the probability of the second event when the events are not independent. In this question, 1 sock has been picked and is not replaced so there is now 1 less to select from when the second sock is picked.

4 **(a)**

1st sock   2nd sock

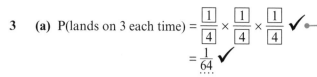

The probabilities on each pair of branches must add up to 1

Marking

Score 1 mark for two or three boxes correct or 2 marks for all boxes correct.

(b) P(black and black) $= \boxed{\dfrac{6}{10}} \times \boxed{\dfrac{5}{9}} = \boxed{\dfrac{30}{90}}$

$\text{P(grey and grey)} = \boxed{\dfrac{4}{10}} \times \boxed{\dfrac{3}{9}} = \boxed{\dfrac{12}{90}}$ ✔

Marking

1 mark if you completed one pair correctly.

P(same colour) = P(black and black) + P(grey and grey) $= \boxed{\dfrac{30}{90}} + \boxed{\dfrac{12}{90}} = \boxed{\dfrac{42}{90}}$ ✔

44 Sampling, averages and range

Write the data in order to find the median score.

$\text{Mean} = \dfrac{\text{sum of data values}}{\text{number of data values}}$

1 **(a)** 4 ✔

(b) $\dfrac{4 + 4 + 9 + 7 + 5 + 2 + 4}{7}$

$\text{Mean} = \dfrac{35}{7} = 5$ ✔

Range = greatest value − least value

Check your answers – the total across should be the same as the total down.

(c) $9 - 2 = 7$ ✔

Marking

1 mark for any three missing values correct and the second mark if all values are correct.

2

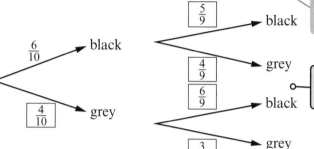

	Adult	Juvenile	Total
Male	81	(39)	120
Female	85	38	(123)
Total	(166)	(77)	(243)

✔ ✔

The mode is the group with the highest frequency.

Core skill

Calculate data value × frequency for each row and then add up these values.
You could add an extra column to your table.

3 **(a)** 2 ✔

(b) $1 \times 5 + 2 \times 9 + 3 \times 8 + 4 \times 6 + 5 \times 2 \ (= 81)$ ✔

$81 \div 30 = 2.7$ ✔

Marking

Score 1 mark for attempting to find the total number of children and 1 mark for the correct final answer.

(c) Because Aaron sampled students, none of the families could have 0 children. ✔

Marking

You could also say that his sample size was small, or that he might have sampled two students from the same family.

4

Mass, x(kg)	Frequency	Midpoint × frequency
$3 \leqslant x < 4$	21	$3.5 \times 21 = 73.5$
$4 \leqslant x < 5$	17	$4.5 \times 17 = 76.5$
$5 \leqslant x < 6$	7	$5.5 \times 7 = 38.5$
$6 \leqslant x < 7$	5	$6.5 \times 5 = 32.5$
Total	50	221

Add an extra column to your table and calculate midpoint × frequency for each class. Don't round your final answer.

✓

$221 \div 50$ ✓

$= 4.42$ kg ✓

Marking

1 mark for multiplying the midpoint of each class by the frequency, 1 mark for dividing your total by the total frequency, and 1 mark for the correct final answer.

45 Representing data

1 **(a)**

Number of pets	Frequency
0	2
1	⑥
2	⑧
3	③
4	1

✓

(b)

Marking

Score 1 mark if the height of your bars matches the frequencies in your table and score the second mark for a complete correct graph including axes labels.

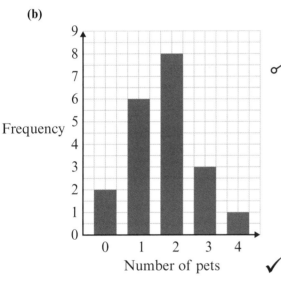

✓ ✓

2 **(a)** 6 ✓

(b) 3 ✓

(c) ✓

Use the key – one picture represents 2 apples.

3 **(a)** red : black

15 : 9

5 : 3 ✓

Write the ratio using the frequencies first, then simplify.

(b) $14 \div 7 = 2$

$2 \times 4 = 8$ ✓

Use the ratio 7 : 4 to work out the value of 1 part, then multiply this to find the value of 4 parts.

46 Representing data (continued)

1 Negative ✔

> The data has a downward trend.

2 **(a), (b)**

> **Core skill**
> You can make predictions from your line of best fit if the prediction is within the range of the data given.

> Draw a line of best fit so it has roughly equal numbers of points on either side.

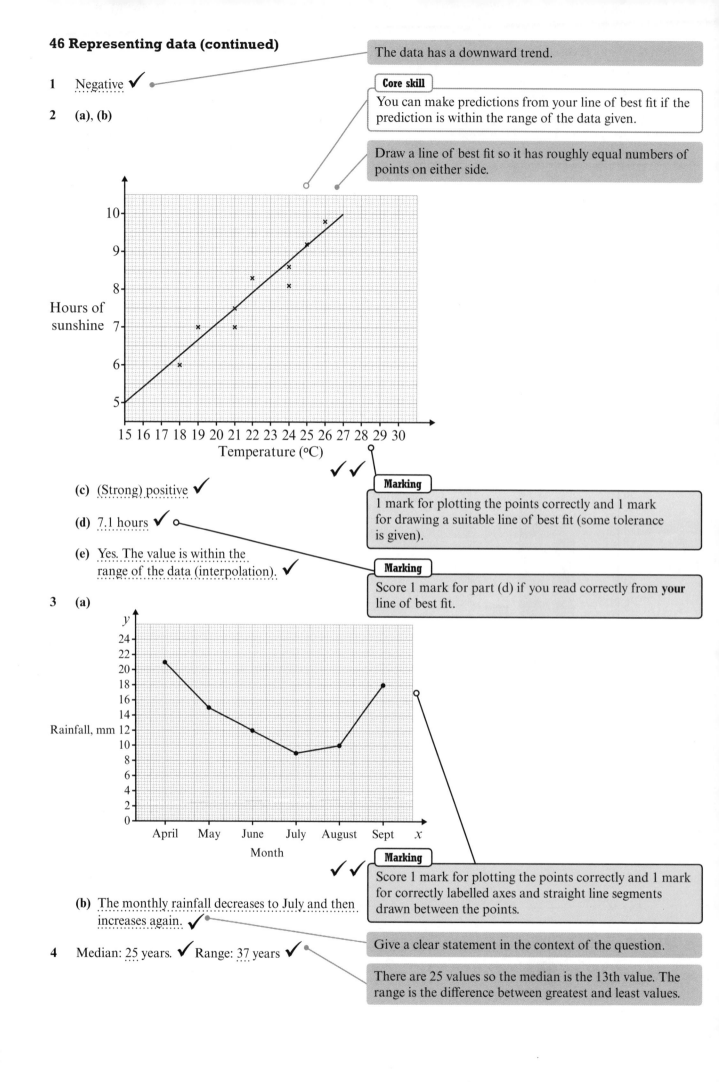

✔ ✔

(c) (Strong) positive ✔

(d) 7.1 hours ✔

> **Marking**
> 1 mark for plotting the points correctly and 1 mark for drawing a suitable line of best fit (some tolerance is given).

(e) Yes. The value is within the range of the data (interpolation). ✔

> **Marking**
> Score 1 mark for part (d) if you read correctly from **your** line of best fit.

3 **(a)**

✔ ✔

> **Marking**
> Score 1 mark for plotting the points correctly and 1 mark for correctly labelled axes and straight line segments drawn between the points.

(b) The monthly rainfall decreases to July and then increases again. ✔

> Give a clear statement in the context of the question.

4 Median: 25 years. ✔ Range: 37 years ✔

> There are 25 values so the median is the 13th value. The range is the difference between greatest and least values.